THE LICENSING HANDBOOK

*An essential guide to obtaining a
licence and running licensed premises*

Nigel Musgrove

Fitzwarren Publishing

©Fitzwarren Publishing 2006

Whilst every care has been taken to ensure the accuracy of this work, no responsibility for loss occasioned to any person acting or refraining from action as a result of any statement in it can be accepted by the author or publisher.

First Edition 1997
Second Edition 2005
Third Edition 2006

British Library Cataloging in Publication Data
A CIP record for this book is available from the British Library.

ISBN 0-9545934 3 X

Published by Fitzwarren Publishing. Printed in UK by Halstan & Co. Ltd

Author's Acknowledgement

To the late Eddie Adams, who dedicated more than a decade, and particularly his last years, to licensing education in Swindon, and to my daughters Suzy, Alisa, and Lizzy, who always keep me smiling.

CONTENTS

1

INTRODUCTION

Alcohol is the central ingredient of this book which provides a guide through the complex regulation of the sale and consumption of this popular drug. For the majority who drink alcohol it is a source of pleasure, a drug which slows down the activity of the central nervous system leading to disinhibition, relaxation, talkativeness and sociability.

Consumption of alcohol can provide great pleasure both in the tasting and the social context in which it takes place, whether it takes place in a pub, club, bar or on some special occasion such as a birthday or wedding.

Alcohol consumption is a central part of the culture of most nations. France has a wine based culture which is integral to the ritual of eating. Consequently the volume consumed and context is different to the United Kingdom, for example, which is essentially a beer drinking culture, often independent of food and often taken in large volumes.

Researchers have also found that in some societies drinkers aggression is commonplace. In others alcohol produces calm humour. But even within these different societies there can be a wide range of alcohol induced behaviour.

Each society has its own unique problems with alcohol. In the United Kingdom today the Government is concerned with the level of binge drinking. It champions a more relaxed "café society" on the continental style, and believes that a relaxation of licensing hours and restrictions on children in licensed premises will encourage this.

In time there may well be a shift in patterns of behaviour but would be unrealistic to expect a speedy change in a culture which is firmly embedded in our national psyche.

In western society binge drinking is predominantly a problem with 18 to 29 year olds. The increase in the past 20 years is directly related to the increased wealth of this age group, their greater disposable income and, perhaps, a taste for excess which has grown out of the 1980s and 1990s.

Invariably binge drinking moderates and disappears as maturity finds such drinkers with increased responsibilities because of jobs and families. Within the problem age group, it is nevertheless clear that the cause of the biggest problem socially is the 18-29 year old club goer.

For an explanation of our current drinking culture we need look no further than the history of our laws to regulate it. Before the creation of Parliament, power lay particularly in the shires and it was in local communities that control existed in accordance with local culture and custom.

With parliamentary democracy in the middle of the second millennium came greater central control driven in part by the recognition that alcohol was a good source of tax. The excuse that higher taxes will also regulate consumption is no truer today than it was in Tudor times.

National licensing laws can be traced back to 1552. All alehouses had to be licensed from 1627.

A fashion for gin was acquired from Holland and could be produced easily and cheaply from English grain. There was an explosion of drunkenness in the late seventeenth century fuelled by the passion for gin. In spite of licensing and a doubling of licence fees and taxes gin consumption increased.

It was not until the end of the eighteenth century that over a hundred years of excess was brought under control by a Royal Proclamation ordering the closure of disorderly or surplus public houses and spirit shops.

In 1828 the Alehouse Act established the General Annual Licensing Meeting of Magistrates who granted Justices Licences for all alehouses. In 1830 the Beer Act provided an opportunity for householders to sell beer without a licence on a single payment of two guineas. This alone provided 25,000 applications within three months. Many of the pubs in our towns and villages today date from that time. This, perhaps, this was the birth of our modern beer drinking culture.

By 1860 all premises involved in the sale of alcohol were brought within the licensing system administered by the magistrates. During this period the Temperance Society was pressing for greater control on the sale and consumption of alcohol. The Society had some success. In 1872 all night opening was prohibited, as was the sale of spirits for consumption on premises to anyone under 16 years old. By 1886 the sale to children under 13 years old of any alcohol for consumption on premises was prohibited

The first major consolidation act, the foundation for a century of licensing law, was the Licensing Act 1910. Different licences were created, such as the victuallers licence ('publicans licence'), beer house licence, cider house licence, and wine licence. Each licence had a limit on the volume which could be sold.

The procedure for applications was established. The legal age for consumption on the premises was raised to 14 years. Since 1908 children under 14 years of age had, with certain exceptions, been prohibited from bars of licensed premises.

It was Lady Astor's Licensing Act of 1923 which raised the age limit to 18 years. It was this Act and its successor, the Act of 1964, which defined the law for the next 80 years.

The new regime for the regulation of the sale and consumption of alcohol in England and Wales is the Licensing Act 2003. It came into force on 24th November 2005 when all previous legislation ceased to have effect.

To summarise the changes brought about by the Act:-

1. Repeal of whole of Licensing Act 1964 and amendment Acts, the Licensing (Occasional Permission) Act 1983, and the relevant section of Local Government (Miscellaneous Provisions) Act 1982. New system of licensing of certain activities namely:-
- ▼ sale by retail of alcohol
- ▼ supply of alcohol by or on behalf of a club to or for a club member
- ▼ provision of regulated entertainment
- ▼ provision of late night refreshment between 11pm and 5am
- ▼ regulated entertainment, ie the provision of entertainment in the presence of an audience for its entertainment consisting of:-
    - a) performance of a play
    - b) exhibition of a film
    - c) indoor sporting event
    - d) boxing or wrestling
    - e) live music
    - f) playing of recorded music
    - g) dance

Regulated entertainment also includes the provision of facilities for participation in e), f) and g). There are some exceptions, for instance incidental music, television or radio broadcasts, entertainment at religious services and places of worship, garden fetes (non profit making), Morris dancing, vehicles in motion.

2. A new licensing authority for all licensable activities – the local authority. The role of the Magistrates' Court is reduced to that of an appeal authority. Licensable activities can be carried out under the following:-
> a) a Premises Licence
> b) a Temporary Event Notice
> c) a Club Premises Certificate

3. Removal of fixed licensing hours

4. Relaxation of controls balanced by rights of police and other authorities together with greater rights for local residents and businesses to challenge a licence at any time and for police to close premises for up to twenty-four hours.

5. Simultaneous extension of police powers to impose fixed penalty fines on under age drinkers, drunks, and those selling alcohol to them.

6. Children: Potential for unlimited access for under 16s provided they are accompanied by an adult (subject to discretion of operator), unless specifically excluded or controlled by condition of Premises Licence.

7. Premises Licences of indefinite duration.

8. Sale of alcohol from premises subject to a Premises Licence must be by or under the authority of the holder of a Personal Licence. Personal Licences have a ten year duration. For each premises used for the sale of alcohol there must be a Designated Premises Supervisor who must hold a Personal Licence.

9. Section 34 Gaming Act 1968: Permits for amusements with machines awarding prizes at venues with a Premises Licence will be

administered by the new licensing authority.

It should be noted that a new Gambling Act 2005 is expected to be in force by the autumn of 2007. This will involve changes to the gaming machine regulations, which have yet to be finalised. It is likely that there will be a maximum number of two machines per premises, unless the licensing authority has on application approved more than two.

Jackpot machines for clubs and miners' welfare institutes under Section 30 and Part III of the Gaming Act 1968 will continue to be administered by the Gaming Committee of the Justices for the relevant petty sessions area. Again the Gambling Act 2005 will introduce changes including licensing authority control and maximum numbers of machines.

10. Temporary Event Notices effectively replace occasional licences and occasional permissions but note that there are limits which could mean that many entertainment venues such as village halls which previously relied on a Public Entertainment Licence will require a Premises Licence. In that case if they also wish to sell alcohol they will require a Designated Premises Supervisor (who must hold a Personal Licence).

11. Licensing objectives which must determine the decisions of licensing authorities, namely:-

> prevention of crime and disorder
> the interests of public safety
> prevention of public nuisance
> protection of children from harm

The government, in their Alcohol Harm Reduction Strategy, promised to review the effects of the new law in 2007. Due to pressure from the media concerned with the effect of the relaxation of licensing hours, the government brought forward the review to the summer of 2006 but missed this target. As a stop gap an interim review of the Guidance was issued in June, with the long awaited substantial review expected in the first quarter of 2007.

There are still major issues with the Licensing Act and regulations which require urgent attention. In particular there is much uncertainty over interpretation of certain areas of the legislation, This especially applies over the role and responsibilities of Designated Premises Supervisors.

The general lack of clarity has led to substantial differences of interpretation between licensing authorities and other responsible authorities such as the police. A Review Panel dealing with fees and costs of the system is already looking at the licensing procedure and has suggested simplification of the licensing process. Expect further changes over the next twelve to eighteen months including a significant increase in fees.

The other major changes which will impact the trade over the next twelve to eighteen months are the smoking ban, expected to be in place in the summer of 2007, and the introduction of the Gambling Act, which is expected to come into force on 1st September 2007.

The trade should also be aware of the changes to fire regulations which came into force from 1st October 2006. Those changes require all operators to carry out their own risk assessments. Also in force from 1st October 2006 is the age discrimination legislation and increased powers of local authorities to deal with noise nuisance at licensed premises.

Every effort has been made to ensure that the information is a correct statement of the law at this time. However as the licensing laws are going through a number of changes and are still subject to possible amendment, some aspects of this book may be out of date at the time of reading itm. It is therefore recommended that anyone with a specific problem should take independent legal advice.

Neither the author nor the publisher can be held liable for losses arising from reliance on information contained in this handbook.

The author thanks all who have commented on the earlier editions and welcomes any further comment from others able to contribute to his quest for accuracy and informed opinion.

Nigel Musgrove - November 2006

2

LICENSABLE ACTIVITIES AND
LICENSING AUTHORITIES

The new Act regulates what are referred to as 'licensable activities' and 'qualifying club activities'. The regulating authority is the licensing authority, and in effect this is the local authority for the area where the premises are to be found.

A. The following licensable activities are regulated by the licensing authority:-

> ▸ the sale by retail of alcohol
> ▸ the supply of alcohol by a club to one of its members
> ▸ the provision of regulated entertainment
> ▸ the provision of late night refreshment

B. The following qualifying club activities are regulated by the licensing authority:-

> ▸ the supply of alcohol by a club to one of its members
> ▸ the sale by retail of alcohol to a club member's guest for consumption on the premises where the sale takes place
> ▸ the provision of regulated entertainment for club members and their guests

Regulated entertainment

This covers entertainment or entertainment facilities, ie facilities enabling people to take part in entertainment, making music or dancing or similar entertainment. Such facilities must be provided for members of the public or a section of the public, exclusively for members of a qualifying club and their guests, or for anyone where a charge is made (and paid by or on behalf of some or all of those entertained) with a view to making a profit.

The following are excluded from the definition of regulated entertain-

ment, and therefore excluded from regulations under the Act:-
- ▸ music incidental to an activity which is not itself a regulated entertainment
- ▸ entertainment at a religious meeting or service or place of public religious worship
- ▸ use of television or radio receivers (but note this means live television/radio. Recorded performances will be regulated)
- ▸ garden fetes unless provided for private gain
- ▸ Morris dancing
- ▸ certain film exhibitions

Included in the definition of regulated entertainment are:-
    a) a performance of a play
    b) an exhibition of a film
    c) an indoor sporting event
    d) boxing or wrestling entertainment
    e) a performance of live music, ie vocal, instrumental or both
    f) any playing of recorded music, ie vocal, instrumental or both
    g) a performance of dance
    h) entertainment similar to e), f) or g)

In each case the entertainment takes place in the presence of an audience for its entertainment. Regulated entertainment also includes the provision of facilities for participation in e), f), g), or h), eg a disco or ballroom dance. To be 'regulated entertainment' the entertainment or facilities must be provided to members of the public or a section of the public or, in the case of a club, for members and their guests, and must be for "consideration with a view to profit".

For this reason private parties at which qualifying entertainment is provided, such as recorded/live music, disco/karaoke facilities now come within regulated entertainment if a charge is made for attendance or use of the facilities or goods or any services are provided. This catches almost any use where the opereator intends to make a profit. The only exemption would be a truly private party where no charge is made or where a charge is made but purely to cover the costs of the entertainment.

Regulated entertainment must also be in the presence of an audience or spectators where the aim is to entertain them. Rehearsals of plays and other performances would not be regulated entertainment unless an audience was invited with a view to profit. A darts match would not be regulated entertainment if an audience spontaneously assembled. However, if it were staged, for example, with celebrity participants with a view to attracting an audience and a view to profit, it would be regulated entertainment as an indoor sporting event.

Late Night Refreshment

The supply of hot food or hot drink to the public between 11pm and 5am on or from premises, no matter where consumption is to take place, but not:-

- ▶ to a hotel resident or his/her guest
- ▶ to a member of a recognised club admitted to the premises in that capacity
- ▶ to someone admitted to the premises in his capacity of an employee of a particular employer
- ▶ to someone in a particular trade, profession or vocation
- ▶ hot drinks which contains alcohol
- ▶ hot drinks from vending machines
- ▶ hot drink or hot food free of charge
- ▶ hot food or hot drink supplied by a registered charity
- ▶ hot food or hot drink supplied on a vehicle at a time when it is not permanently or temporarily parked (ie when in motion)

Many pubs hotels and restaurants have been caught out by this development. It was really aimed at the late night food market, the hot food vans and takeaways which invariably serve late night revellers and are a part of the late night economy.

Hotels will usually be exempt, but not if they allow non-residents (who are not guests of a resident) to use their facilities. Hotels are advised to ensure that they are fully covered for Late Night Refreshment.

For late night food vans and other premises the changes have been traumatic, particularly where they were previously not subject to local government control.

9

Many premises which had operated for decades found themselves with no protected rights on application for new Premises Licences. Local residents who had seen them as a nuisance also saw an opportunity to control or rid themselves of such premises.

Some licensing authorities imposed their own agendas. As a result many applicants, to their surprise, found themselves with licences which undermined their commercial viability.

C. Licensing Objectives

The licensing authority is the local authority, whether it be the district council or county council where there are no district councils, county or county borough in Wales, London Borough Council, or Council of the City of London. Its main task is to promote the following objectives:-

 ▶ the prevention of crime and disorder
 ▶ ensure public safety
 ▶ the prevention of public nuisance
 ▶ the protection of children from harm

Licensing authorities consult the police, fire authority, business and residents' representatives in their area and then publish a Licensing Statement, a policy document which runs for three years. In furthering their objectives the licensing authority must bear in mind its published Licensing Statement and the Guidance issued by the Secretary of State (see later in this chapter).

A licensing committee of at least ten but not more than 15 members conducts the business of a licensing authority. The committee may establish one or more sub-committees consisting of a miniumum of three members.

The sub-committee may discharge any of the authority's functions and officers may be delegated to discharge some functions although there is a long list of functions which cannot be delegated to an officer.

D. Guidance and Licensing Statements

The Guidance, approved by Parliament, does not override the Licensing Act. It is intended to help licensing authorities strike a balance between greater freedom and flexibility for the leisure industry and increased powers of the police and licensing authorities to protect residents from disturbance.

The authority need not follow the Guidance but it must "have regard" to it. Where the authority does not follow the Guidance it must justify its decision. A licensing authority must have regard to the Guidance when making and publishing its Licensing Statement. Before determining its Licensing Statement the licensing authority must consult:-

▶ the chief officer of police for the area
▶ the fire authority
▶ representatives of local holders of Premises Licences
▶ representatives of local holders of Club Premises Certificates
▶ representatives of local holders of Personal Licences
▶ representatives of businesses and residents in its area
▶ prior to making its first Licensing Statement, representatives of current licence holders

The views of those consulted must be given appropriate weight but it is for the licensing authority to decide on the full extent of consultation.

Licensing Statements should make it clear that conditions will concentrate on matters within the control of individual licensees, on "the direct impact of activities taking place at the licensed premises on members of the public living, working or engaged in normal activity in the area concerned".

The old regime saw the cumulative impact of a concentration of licensed premises cause particular social problems. Whilst licensing authorities should consider such impact in the context of the promotion of the licensing objectives (for example the prevention of crime and disorder, public safety, and the prevention of public nuisance) the Guidance emphasises that "the individual merits of each application must always be considered".

Quotas should not be imposed which restrict consideration of an application on its merits or seek to impose limitations on trading hours. In some areas it may be necessary for licensing authorities to adopt a policy of refusing new licences for a specific area but each application should be considered on its merits. It is for the licensing authority to show that the grant would undermine the promotion of one of the licensing objectives, with or without necessary conditions.

A special saturation policy adopted by a licensing authority should apply only to applications for new premises, and should not justify or include conditions for a terminal hour in any area. Zoning, the setting of fixed trading hours within an area, should not be adopted as a policy.

As far as shops, stores and supermarkets are concerned, the Guidance strongly recommends such premises be allowed to provide off sales at any time they are open for shopping.

Conditions duplicating other legislation, such as that concerning fire or health and safety at work, cannot be necessary for the promotion of the licensing objectives. Standard conditions should be avoided but model 'pools of conditions' are acceptable provided that they are tailored to the individual premises or event.

Many authorities have been challenged on their statements of licensing policy. One authority to find itself in court was Canterbury City Council, the High Court delivering its judgment in June 2005.

The court made it clear that where an application did not provoke relevant representations (see chapters 3 and 13), an applicant was entitled to the grant of a licence with conditions consistent with the operating schedule put forward in the application and any mandatory conditions but no more.

Canterbury City Council's policy was deemed unlawful in that it suggested that its requirements would be imposed on the contents of the application and additional conditions would apply whether or not the application was met with formal opposition.

There are other examples of questionable licensing policies. Court challenges may be expected over the coming few years which should clarify many issues.

Some authorities believe that they can impose conditions requiring the Designated Premises Supervisor to be present on the premises at all times when alcohol is sold. Others believe they can require a Personal Licence holder to be present at all times when alcohol is sold.

Both go far beyond what is set out in the Licensing Act and indeed the Guidance.

On the matter of delegation, the Guidance recommends the following which acknowledges what, under the Licensing Act, can be delegated and to whom. The Licensing Statement may only be dealt with by a full committee but all the following may be delegated as follows:-

Application/determination	Sub C'ttee	Officers
Personal Licence	If objection made	If no objection made
Personal Licence with unspent convictions	All cases	
Premises Licence/Club Premises Certificate	If represent'n made	If no represent'n made
Provisional Statement	If represent'n made	If no represent'n made
Vary Premises Licence/Club Premises Certificate	If represent'n made	If no represent'n made
Vary Designated Premises Supervisor	If a police object	All other cases
Removal as Designated Premises Supervisor		All cases
Transfer of Premises Licence	If police object	All other cases
InterimAuthorities	If police object	All other cases
Review Premises Licence /Club Premises Certificate	All cases	
Whether a complaint is irrelevant frivolous vexatious etc		All cases
Objection when local auth'ty consulted is not relevant auth'ty considering applic'n	All cases	
Determination of police objection to Temporary Event Notice	All cases	

The Guidance runs to over 160 pages. Relevant subjects will be covered later in the appropriate chapters, eg Premises Licences, Club Premises Certificates, and Personal Licences.

3

PREMISES LICENCES

A Premises Licence will be required if the premises (any place including the open air) are to be used for a licensable activity. Application is made to the licensing authority for the area in which the premises are situated. The licence can be permanent or for a limited period of time.

An applicant must be 18 years or over. An applicant must be either:-

1) a person carrying on or intending to carry on a business which involves the use of the premises for any of the licensable activities
2) a recognised club
3) a charity
4) the proprietor of an educational institution
5) a health service body
6) a person registered for an independent hospital
7) a chief officer of police

Person includes a limited company, business or partnership. It is not necessary for an individual to hold a Premises Licence.

Regulations set out the procedure, the forms to be used, and the fees.

Procedure for application for a new Premises Licence

1. Application must be made on the proper form.
2. It must be accompanied by:-
   a) the fee
   b) an operating schedule in the proper form (contained in the application form or annexed)
   c) a plan to a scale of 1:100 metric complying with the regulations.
   d) if the licensable activities include the supply of alcohol, a form of consent in the proper form by the person who will be the premises supervisor, ie the person given day to day responsibility for running the premises

14

3. The application and accompanying documents must be served on the licensing authority and on the same day on the following authorities, known as responsible authorities:-

> the chief of police for the area
> the fire authority for the area
> the enforcing authority for the area under the Heath and Safety at Work Act
> the planning authority for the area
> the environmental health officer for the area
> the recognised body in the area for the representation of child protection agencies (most likely to be the Social Services)
> the local weights and measures authority
> where relevant, The British Waterways Board

Where applications are being sent by post, it is best to despatch them at the same time by special delivery in order to be certain of the day of service. This is crucial to the time limits for insertion in the display notice and to calculate the time limits for display and advertisement.

4. The application must be advertised in the proper form by display and newspaper advertisement. Regulations specify the size, colour and content of the notice for display, as well as the print size, font and where the notice must be placed, ie A4 or larger, pale blue with black print, font size 16 or larger. The notice should include a detailed description of the licensable activities and, where the application is for a variation, it must include the hours applied for, but this is advisable on any application.

5. The notice of advertisement must be on display for 28 working days starting the day after the notice of application was given to the licensing authority. The advertisement must appear in a local newspaper within ten working days calculated from the day after the notice of application was given to the licensing authority. Some authorities require a copy of the advertisement to be sent to them within a certain time limit. Although this is not a legal requirement, it is recommended as good practice.

The Review Panel has recommended simplifying the advertisement process, possibly with a requirement for notices to be put into free newspapers and other publications and for letters to be sent to neighbouring residents. This last recommendation may create more problems than it solves but it remains to be seen how the government reacts.

6. Fees: the fee for applications for new licences is based on the non-domestic rateable value (NDRV) of the premises. There is in addition an annual fee payable based on the NDRV. The formula is:-

NDRV bands
A: 0 to £4,300   B: £4,301 to £33,000
C: £33,001 to £87,000   D: £87,001 to £125,000
E: £125,001 and above

Fees:

Bands	A	B	C	D	E
Main Application Fee	100	190	315	450	635
Main annual charge	70	180	295	320	350

There are exceptions in which case fees are significantly higher. The first exception is where the premises, not being purpose built or modified structures, have a capacity of 5,000 or more. In such cases the scale of fees is between £1,000 and £64,000. In the main this will apply to outdoor events.

The most significant exception applies to premises in bands D or E. If the premises are used exclusively or primarily for the supply and consumption of alcohol then band D fees are doubled, band E trebled. In that case band D fees will be £900 for a main application, with an annual charge of £640. Band E fees will be £1,905 with an annual charge of £1,050.

There is no explanation of the term 'exclusively or primarily used'. Clearly it will not apply to hotels, bingo halls, cinemas, theatres and restaurants. It will apply to the so called 'vertical drinking' venues where alcohol is the main commodity sold.

If food or entertainment is a significant part of the business these enhanced fees should not be payable but as there is no definition of the term it may have to wait for a court ruling before the position can be fully clarified.

Fees are paid on application and thereafter on the anniversary of the grant. The Review Panel has recommended that this should be changed to a set annual renewal/payment date. The Review Panel is charged with examining whether the current fee structure covers the full cost of the authorities' administration of their licensing duties. It is likely that costs have far outstripped the government's own initial assessments on which the fees were based and significant increases in fees may be expected in the future.

7. The operating schedule is an essential part of the application and is provided for in the forms which must be used. It defines the extent of activities to be carried on. It will set the scene with a general description of the style and character of the premises and the entertainment to be provided. It must give details of the proposed licensable activities; the times when they are to take place, the times the premises are open to the public, the period of the licence.

It must identify where the supply of alcohol and any other licensable activities will take place. It must identify whether alcohol is supplied for consumption on or off the premises or both and it must, where alcohol is to be supplied, give the name and address of the proposed Designated Premises Supervisor. It should also identify any steps to be taken to promote the four licensing objectives.

It is strongly recommended that an applicant consult all the responsible authorities as part of a risk assessment before submitting an application. It will help if reference is made to the model standard conditions, which can be found in the Guidance. Where relevant, conditions should be offered.

Whilst it is recommended that the application should address issues and requirements set out in the Guidance and the relevant authority's licensing policy statement, there is no legal obligation to carry out, for example, risk assessments or to comply with any requirements which go beyond the matters set out in the Licensing Act and regulations (see the Canterbury case referred to in chapter 2).

If there are relevant representations these matters should be addressed as they will undoubtedly attract the attention of the authority at the hearing, but it is for the applicant to decide how he wishes to approach any hearing, bearing in mind known representations (see chapter 12 on notices and hearings).

8. Plans must be to a scale of 1:100 on the metric scale (endorsed on the plan) unless the licensing authority has agreed beforehand in writing an alternative scale with the applicant.

The plans must contain the following information, if convenient by way of symbols and colouring with a legend:-

a) the extent of the boundary of the building and external and internal walls

b) the perimeter of the premises, to include gardens and grounds used for licensable activities

c) entries, exits and escape routes

d) the areas to be used for each activity where more than one licensable activity is to be carried out

d) fixed structures and objects including fixed furniture which may impede emergency evacuation

d) the location and height of any stage or raised areas

e) the location of steps, stairs, elevators and lifts

f) the location of rooms containing public conveniences

g) the location of fire safety equipment, including fire extinguishers, fire doors, emergency lighting and fire alarms

h) the location of any kitchen

The regulations on plans have proved to be unduly strict and consequently expensive. The damage has mostly been done but for future applications it is likely that more relaxed requirements will be introduced on recommendation of the Review Panel.

9. When the authority, having received an application, is satisfied that the relevant procedural requirements have been met and there are no relevant representations, the authority must grant the licence as applied for and can only impose conditions which are:-

▶ consistent with the operating schedule – this usually means those offered by the applicant

▶ mandatory conditions set out in the Act (see later in this chapter)

10. If the licensing authority receives relevant representations, it must hold a hearing within 20 working days beginning the day after the

period for representations expires, (see item 11) unless the authority, applicant and all those making representations agree. It must then decide whether to:-

> ▸ grant the licence subject to conditions consistent with the operating schedule and the mandatory conditions
>
> ▸ grant the licence with modified conditions it considers necessary for the promotion of the licensing objectives and subject to the mandatory conditions
>
> ▸ exclude from the scope of the licence any of the required licensing activities
>
> ▸ refuse to specify a person in the licence as Designated Premises Supervisor
>
> ▸ reject the application

11. Relevant representations relate to the likely effect of a Premises Licence on the promotion of the licensing objectives. They must be made by an interested party or responsible authority within 28 consecutive days beginning the day after the authority received the application. Each representation must not, in the opinion of the authority, be either frivolous or vexatious. The test is an objective one. Would an ordinary and reasonable person consider the representation vexatious or frivolous?

12. Interested parties are those living in the vicinity of the premises, a body representing persons who live in that vicinity, a person involved in a business in that vicinity, or a body representing such persons. A person includes a business or partnership. There is no legal definition of "vicinity".

Much will depend upon the area in question. In a built up city centre vicinity may be no more than a few hundred yards. In a country village it may be a square mile or more. In a case before Birmingham magistrates on appeal the court decided that a resident who lived 150 yards away from a city centre premises was not in the vicinity of it.

The government has issued guidance for interested parties wishing to make representations and this can be found on the DCMS website at http://www.culture.gov.uk/NR/rdonlyres/9F1334B2-09E7-44D7-AE74-D00618EF5F02/0/Guidancemakingrepresentations.pdf.

13. Responsible authorities see item 3

14. Decision: Upon granting or rejecting a Premises Licence application the authority must without delay give notice to the applicant, to any person who made representations, and to the police. Where the licence is granted and representations made or rejected the authority must also state in the notice the reasons for its decision. A disappointed applicant or person who made representations may appeal (see chapter 11).

Conditions

The mandatory conditions relate to licences authorising the supply of alcohol, films, and those requiring security by individuals.

Alcohol: Supply of alcohol under the Premises Licence must be made or authorised by a person holding a Personal Licence. Such a person need not be physically present as he/she can authorise staff to make sales, but the government warns that it is for the courts to decide whether the frequency or period of absence mean that a sale could not be authorised. It is recommended that all staff be given written authority by name and a copy of that authority be kept on the premises.

No supply of alcohol may be made at a time when there is no Designated Premises Supervisor (DPS) or that DPS does not hold a Personal Licence or his Personal Licence is suspended.

Films: Admission of children must be restricted in accordance with the recommendation of a designated film classification body, and in some circumstances the licensing authority.

Door Supervision: With some limited exceptions, if the Premises Licence includes a provision that security staff must be employed, there must be a further condition that they are licensed by the Security Industry Authority.

Other conditions may only be imposed on Premises Licences where they are necessary for the promotion of the four licensing objectives. For more on conditions see chapter 5.

Designated Premises Supervisors (DPS)

The Guidance makes it clear that the main purpose of the DPS is to make sure that there is a readily identifiable person who has day-to-day responsibility for running the premises. The Act does not define the duties and responsibilities of the DPS, a glaring omission as the Guidance refers to them.

The government has attempted to clear the air in the Interim Review issued in June 2006, but is still does not go far enough. The statement indicates that a DPS may supervise more than one premises so long as he/she is able to ensure that the four licensing objectives will be properly promoted on those premises and that licensing law and licence conditions will be complied with.

The DPS must hold a Personal Licence. The Guidance makes it clear that the police should only object to a DPS in exceptional circumstances. For more information on the DPS refer to chapter 6.

Duration of Licence

A Premises Licence remains in force until it is either revoked, surrendered or, if it was granted for a limited period, that period expires.

However, if it is suspended it has no effect during the period of supervision. A surrender is effected by the holder of the Premises Licence giving notice of surrender to the licensing authority. The licence itself must accompany the notice or a reason given why it is not produced. Anyone with a property interest, such as a landlord or secured lender, can protect themselves by registering their interest with the licensing authority, but this must be renewed annually, and there is a fee to pay.

Registration entitles such a person to immediate notification by the licensing authority of any change to the register. Should any change occur, they will only have a short time to act (see later in this chapter).

In the case of death, mental incapacity, insolvency or dissolution of the holder, or a club ceasing to be recognised, the licence will lapse. In certain circumstances, where a licence has lapsed because of one of these events or surrender, it can be kept alive or reinstated (see later).

Loss of Premises Licence

In the event of loss of the Premises Licence or summary, the holder may apply to the licensing authority for a copy on payment of the fee of £10.50. The authority must issue a copy if it is satisfied that the original has been lost, stolen, damaged or destroyed, and that where it has been lost or stolen the holder has reported the loss or theft to the police.

Provisional Statement

Where the premises are not yet built, or extension or alterations are planned or under way it would be useful and often financially necessary to have some prior indication from the licensing authority that a Premises Licence will be granted when the work is completed.

The way to obtain this is to apply for a Provisional Statement. Such a statement, however, does not guarantee that a Premises Licence will be granted or that it will be in the same terms as the Provisional Statement. If possible it may be advisable to apply for a Premises Licence, which will require clear plans, an operating schedule, and the proposed DPS. Otherwise a Provisional Statement is the only alternative.

An applicant for a Provisional Statement must be over 18 years old and have an interest in the premises. An application must be in the proper form and accompanied by the fee of £315 and a schedule of works consisting of details of the premises, the proposed licensable activities, and plans of the proposed works. The application must be advertised. See earlier in this chapter for details of display and advertisement.

Where the licensing authority receives an application and it is satisfied that the application has been properly advertised, it must issue the applicant with a provisional statement provided that there are no relevant representations. If there are such representations the authority must hold a hearing (unless the applicant and each person making a representation agree that a hearing is unnecessary).

For definitions of relevant representations, interested party and responsible authority see earlier in this chapter. The licensing authority must determine, faced with an application for a Premises Licence, whether on completion of the works it will:-

> ‣ grant the licence subject to conditions consistent with the operating schedule and the mandatory conditions
> ‣ grant the licence with modified conditions it considers necessary for the promotion of the licensing objectives and the mandatory conditions

22

‣ exclude any of the required licensable activities
‣ reject the application

The licensing authority must then issue the applicant with a statement giving details of its decision and reasons for any grant with modifications or exclusions. It must also give a copy to the police and each person who made a representation.

Where an application is for a Premises Licence for premises for which a Provisional Statement has been issued and if it is in the same form as the licence described in the Provisional Statement and the work has been satisfactorily completed, representations will be excluded if the person making the representations could have made the same or substantially the same representation about the application for the Provisional Statement but did not do so and has no reasonable excuse.

It is difficult to know what will be accepted as a reasonable excuse. Representations will be allowed if there has been any material change relating either to the premises or to the area in the vicinity since the Provisional Statement was made. There is no definition of "material change", and no help in the Guidance. While a Provisional Statement does provide encouragement that a similar Premises Licence will be granted it is no guarantee.

Variation of Premises Licences

The holder of a Premises Licence can apply to the licensing authority if he wishes to vary the licence. However, a licence may not be varied to extend any period for which it has effect or to "vary substantially" the premises. Until June 2006 there was no guidance on what precisely was meant by "vary substantially".

The interim review stated rather harshly that a major variation is one that is not a change in name or address of someone named in the licence. This means that any structural alteration however small, for example change in the position or size of a bar structure, will require a full blown application for a variation. Some licensing authorities are adopting a sensible approach and just requiring a deposit of amended plans where other responsible authorities have no objections, but other licensing authorities are adopting a strict approach.

Hopefully the government will deal with this and provide a clear and cost effective solution when the full review of the Guidance is published in 2007.

The application must be served on the licensing authority. As usual there is a proper form and the fee is calculated in the same way as an application for a new licence.

The application must be advertised in accordance with regulations. The application and documents; the plan of the premises complying with the regulations; the Premises Licence, or a statement giving the reason for failure to provide it; and the fee must be given to the licensing authority and at the same time served on the responsible authorities. For plans, advertisements and fees, see points 4, 5, 6 and 8 earlier in this chapter.

If the licensing authority is satisfied that the application has been properly advertised it must grant the application unless relevant representations are made. For definitions of relevant representations, interested party and responsible authority refer to earlier sections in this chapter.

The time for representations and a hearing are the same as set out in earlier in this chapter. When there are relevant representations the licensing authority must hold a hearing within 20 working days beginning the day after the 28 day period for representations expires, unless the applicant and each person making a representation agree a hearing is unnecessary.

The authority may reject the whole or part of the application, or may modify the conditions of the licence by altering, omitting or adding conditions as it considers necessary for the promotion of the licensing objectives.

There is a danger that in submitting an application for variation, unwanted conditions may be imposed or the Premises Licence restricted. As with the grant of a Premises Licence, notice must be given and where representations are made the applicant and anyone making a representation as well as the police, must be notified of the reasons for any decision.

Variation of Premises Supervisor

The holder of a Premises Licence, which allows the sale of alcohol, must remember that for such sales to take place there must be a DPS who holds a Personal Licence. If the person identified in the Premises

24

Licence as the DPS has his Personal Licence revoked or suspended, it will be necessary for the holder of the Premises Licence to act quickly if he is to avoid an enforced alcohol free period of trading or conviction.

A similar position will arise if the DPS ceases to have any connection with the premises, thus necessitating a replacement, or if the DPS gives notice to the licensing authority that he is no longer willing to hold the post.

The holder of a Premises Licence may apply to the licensing authority to vary the licence to name a replacement DPS. There is a specified form of application and fee of £23. An application must be accompanied by a form of consent from the proposed DPS, and the Premises Licence or, if not practicable, a statement giving the reason for not providing it.

Notice of the application must be given on the same day to the police and the outgoing DPS. The notice must say if it is to have immediate effect.The police have 14 days from notification to decide whether to object and may only do so if they are satisfied that there are exceptional circumstances which mean that granting the application would undermine the crime prevention objective.

If the application indicates that it is to have immediate effect, it will do so from the time it is received by the licensing authority until the time the application is withdrawn, rejected, or stated to take effect. Where no objections are received from the police the licensing authority must grant the application.

Where the police do object within the time limit the licensing authority must hold a hearing within 20 working days beginning the day after the 14 day period for representations expires, unless the applicant and police agree that a hearing is unnecessary.

The authority must reject the application if it considers such action necessary for the promotion of the crime prevention objective. Notice of the decision must be given to the applicant, the police, and the proposed supervisor and, where the police have made objection, the licensing authority must give reasons for their decision.

In the case of grant, the notice must specify when it is to take effect.The holder of the Premises Licence must immediately notify the outgoing DPS of the grant and in the case of rejection he must notify the DPS that he remains in post. Failure to do so without reasonable excuse is a criminal offence.

Withdrawal by Designated Premises Supervisor

If a DPS wants to stop being the supervisor for the premises he can serve a notice on the licensing authority in the prescribed form. If he is also the holder of the Premises Licence, the notice must be accompanied by the licence or if not practicable a statement of reasons for non-production.

He will cease being the DPS on receipt of the notice by the licensing authority or later if the notice provides for a later time. Within 48 hours of giving the notice a copy must be served by the DPS on the Premises Licence holder with a notice requiring him to send to the licensing authority within 14 days either the licence or a statement why it is not practicable to do so. Failure by the Premises Licence holder to comply is a criminal offence.

The danger here for Premises Licence holders is obvious. An aggrieved DPS could leave the licence holder unaware of withdrawal for 48 hours during which time alcohol may have been sold unlawfully.

Someone with a property interest can protect themselves but surprisingly not the Premises Licence holder. Urgent action may be necessary to vary the DPS. It is recommended that Premises Licence holders are prepared for this potential problem. It is a good idea to have at least two Personal Licence holders per premises.

A readily prepared form for varying the DPS and a form of consent from the proposed DPS can be kept handy for such an emergency but it will be necessary for hand delivery to the licensing authority as sending a fax or an email is of no use since the notice does not take effect until the licensing authority receives the fee.

If prompt action is taken on becoming aware of the resignation of the DPS it is unlikely that any prosecution would follow regarding sale of alcohol in the intervening period.

Duty to notify change of name or address

The Premises Licence holder must "as soon as is reasonably practicable", notify the licensing authority of any change of his name or address. He must also notify the authority of any change of name and address of the DPS where that supervisor has not done so. The notice must be accompanied by the fee of £10.50 and the Premises Licence or statement giving the reason for failure to produce.

Currently there is no obligation on the DPS to notify either the licensing authority or the holder of the Premises Licence of any change of name or address. The supervisor may voluntarily give notice, and in that case he must give a copy to the Premises Licence holder. The holder of the Premises Licence will commit an offence if he fails to notify changes of name or address without reasonable excuse. It must be presumed that failure by the DPS to inform the Premises Licence holder will be a reasonable excuse!

Transfer of Premises Licences

A transfer of the Premises Licence may be necessary, for example, where the ownership of the premises or business has changed hands.Where a change is planned it is important to act in advance in order to identify the proposed DPS. The procedure for transfer is similar to all applications. There is a form to be completed and it must be served on the licensing authority together with:-

▶ the Premises Licence
▶ the consent of the outgoing licence holder
▶ fee of £23
▶ and, where a change in DPS is taking place, the application for variation and consent of the proposed DPS

The application and accompanying documents must be given on the same day to the police and the current DPS. The police have 14 days in which to object and they can only do so if they are satisfied that in the exceptional circumstances the proposed transfer would undermine the crime prevention objective, as when for example the business or individuals involved are concerned in crime.

If the authority receives an objection in time it must hold a hearing within 20 working days of the end of the period for receipt of objections unless the objection is withdrawn or it is agreed a hearing is unnecessary.

The police must prove their case and if they do the application must be rejected. Where there is no objection and all the paperwork is in order the transfer must be granted. However, the applicant could ask for the transfer to have interim effect from the date of receipt by the licensing authority. This, together with any associated change of DPS, should be timed to coincide with the completion of the business purchase.

In this case the interim effect will last until the transfer application is rejected withdrawn or granted. This will cover a situation where trading will continue on changeover of ownership and it is necessary to obtain authority to continue the licensable activities pending formal transfer. It is recommended that advance contact is made with the police to ensure they will not object to the proposed Premises Licence holder and DPS.

When an application is granted or rejected the licensing authority must notify the applicant and police. If there were police objections reasons for the grant must be given. The notice must also state when the transfer is to take effect and a copy must be given to the previous holder. Both the incoming and outgoing DPS must be notified immediately.

Transfers and Interim Authority Notices in the case of death, mental incapacity, insolvency and surrender

A Premises Licence lapses automatically and immediately if the holder of the licence dies, becomes mentally incapable, insolvent or is dissolved, or if the licence is surrendered. It is very important that immediate action is taken to keep alive the licence if it is intended to continue trading or protect the business for sale.

In the case of surrender, anyone with a property interest, such as a landlord, who has registered an interest, will be notified by the licensing authority. Anyone qualified to apply for a Premises Licence may, within seven days of the licence lapsing, apply for the transfer of the licence provided they also ask for it to have interim effect. The application will re-instate the Premises Licence from the time the authority receives both the paperwork in order and the relevant fee.

Only one application may be made and in the case of rejection the licence will lapse. Otherwise the procedure on transfer applications explained earlier in this chapter will apply.

In the case of death, incapacity and insolvency, there are two options. Anyone qualified to apply for a Premises Licence could apply for a transfer and the licence will be reinstated until the application is determined. However, a spouse, personal representative, holder of an enduring power of attorney, or insolvency practitioner may wish merely to continue trading until the sale or disposal of the business. If this is the case such a person can give an interim authority notice. This must be given to the licensing authority within seven days of the lapse of the Premises Licence, together with the fee of £23.

On the same day the notice must be given to the police. What this will mean in practice, for example, is that if a Premises Licence holder dies on a Saturday the licensing authority must be in receipt of the notice and fee by the following Friday at the latest, giving only four working days to deal with the application at a most traumatic time.

The interim notice will take effect immediately the notice and fee are received by the licensing authority and will be valid for two months. Beyond that date it will be necessary to apply for a full transfer to have immediate interim effect, as only one interim authority notice can be given.

The police can object to an interim authority notice by giving notice but must establish exceptional circumstances that pose a real threat to the crime prevention objective. To object police must give notice within 48 hours of receiving the interim authority notice.

A hearing must be held within five working days beginning the day after the 48 hour period for objection expires, unless everyone agrees otherwise. If the licensing authority agrees with the police they must cancel the notice. Cancellation will take effect on receipt of formal notice with reasons for the decision. An interim authority notice cannot be cancelled if application has been made for a full transfer with interim effect.

A person who becomes the holder of a Premises Licence by interim authority notice must immediately notify the DPS, failure to do so being a criminal offence.

Review of Premises Licence

The Guidance sets out the purpose of the review provisions as a "key protection for the community where problems associated with crime and disorder, public safety, public nuisance or the protection of children from harm are occurring". A wide range of people and organisations can apply for a review. The full list is:-

    Police
    Fire authority

Health and Safety authority
Planning authority
Environmental Health authority
Child Protection Agency representative
Weights and Measures Authority (Trading Standards Officer)
Person living in the vicinity or representative body eg residents'
  association
Business in the vicinity or representative body

Licensing authorities themselves cannot start a review procedure, but other local authority officers listed above can intervene. The Guidance makes it clear that licensing authorities should treat applications for new licences and variations leniently as there is a robust review procedure in place. It encourages a partnership between applicants, agencies and local communities, with consultation at an early stage. The review procedure should be a last resort.

It is important for everyone concerned to communicate and tackle problems immediately they arise. Early co-operation and action should prevent the need for any application for review. However, it is important for all who may be involved with a review, Premises Licence holders, responsible authorities such as the police or environmental health authority, local residents and businesses that they keep records of all incidents, complaints and actions as these records may be vital evidence in any review hearing.

Regulations set out the notice, time and method of service, and the requirement for advertisement. When a review notice is received the licensing authority will first check whether it is relevant to one of the four licensing objectives and that it is given by a valid objector. If the request for a review originates from an individual rather than a relevant authority or body, the authority will also ensure it is not frivolous, vexatious or a repetition of an earlier application.

The Guidance recommends that there should be not more than one review on similar grounds in a 12 month period, unless there are exceptional circumstances or there has been a closure order. Valid grounds for review must be submitted to a hearing and the licensing authority has power to modify the licence conditions; exclude a licensable activity (eg the playing of live music) permanently or for up to three months; remove the DPS; suspend the licence for up to three months; or revoke the licence.

The Guidance stresses that any detrimental financial impact must be necessary and proportionate to the promotion of the licensing objectives.

To coincide with the introduction of the Act in November 2005 the government issued several informal guidances. They are informal to the extent that they themselves do not have statutory effect. They include guidance to interested parties applying for a Review.

They can be accessed on the DCMS website at http://www.culture .gov.uk/NR/rdonlyres/A2DBCE6D-CC18-40DD-A2E7- 315940A4A599/0/GuidanceReviews.pdf

The decision and reasons must be notified to all parties and does not take effect until either the end of the period for appeal (21 days from notification) or outcome of an appeal. There is talk that the government may introduce an amendment enforcing a decision with immediate effect, which may be somewhat harsh on a premises operator who may go out of business or at best suffer severe financial loss before any appeal is heard.

Inspection of Premises

A police officer, licensing officer, fire officer, health and safety or environmental health officer, may at any reasonable time enter the premises for assessment of an application for a new Premises Licence, provisional statement, variation or review. A police officer may, if necessary, use force. It is a criminal offence to intentionally obstruct such entry.

Maintaining, keeping, displaying and producing the Premises Licence

The licensing authority has a duty to make appropriate amendments to the licence and can call on the holder to produce it within 14 days. Failure to do so without reasonable excuse is an offence.

The holder must keep the licence or certified copy at the premises either under his control, or under the control of someone who works there who has been nominated in writing as the keeper. He must also prominently display the summary of the licence or a certified copy with a notice identifying the person nominated as the keeper of the licence.

Any copy must be certified by the licensing authority, a solicitor or notary. A suggested notice can be found at the end of this chapter. Failure to comply with these requirements is a criminal offence.

A police officer, licensing officer, fire officer, health and safety or environmental health officer, may request production of the Premises Licence for examination, and failure to comply without reasonable excuse is an offence.

Registered Interests

Anyone with a property interest, such as a landlord or secured lender, can protect himself by registering his interest with the licensing authority but this must be renewed annually and there is a fee to pay of £21.

Registration entitles the registrant to immediate notification by the licensing authority of any change to the register. After notification the registrant has only a matter of days to take action.

Suggested notice identifying nominated keeper of Premises Licence

Licensing Act 2003 - Section 57(3)

I/We [   ] being the holder of the Premises Licence for [   ] situated at [   ] give notice that [   ] who works at the premises and who holds the position of [   ] is the person nominated to have custody or control at the premises of the Premises Licence and Summary or certified copies of those documents.

Date:...........................

Signed:...........................
Premises Licence Holder/Director of Premises Licence Holder

4

CLUBS

Proprietary clubs will need a Premises Licence, as profits normally go to the owners rather than members. Genuine members' clubs can apply for a Club Premises Certificate. There are also provisions which treat registered friendly societies and provident societies and miners' welfare institutes as members' clubs.

The main advantage of a Club Premises Certificate is that there is no need for a Designated Premises Supervisor (DPS), and therefore no need for anyone to hold a Personal Licence. No licensing qualifications are necessary.

A club requires a Club Premises Certificate to carry on a qualifying club activity, namely:-

1) the supply of alcohol to members for consumption on or off the premises where the supply takes place.

2) the sale of alcohol to a guest of a member for consumption on the premises where the sale takes place. Guest includes an associate member and a guest of that member. A person is an associate member if the club rules allow admission as a member of another registered club, ie a club which satisfies the general conditions mentioned below.

The difficulty any club will face here is that its officials may not know - and have no easy means of finding out - if another club satisfies the conditions, such as whether it is established and conducted in good faith.

There may be a particular problem with visiting sporting teams. Team members may not belong to a club which satisfies the general conditions. The Act does not retain the general waiver for members of visiting sporting teams but there may be a way around this if clubs make provision in their rules for visiting teams to be classed as guests. For more on this see below.

3) the provision of regulated entertainment for members of the club and their guests. Regulated entertainment is one or more of the following activities entertaining an audience:-

> ▸ performance of a play
> ▸ showing of a film
> ▸ indoor sporting event
> ▸ boxing or wrestling
> ▸ live music
> ▸ recorded music
> ▸ dance
> ▸ facilities for members and their guests to make music, sing
>   or dance

For a more detailed consideration of regulated entertainment see chapter 2.

A Club Premises Certificate may not authorise the supply of alcohol to members for consumption off the premises unless it has three conditions attached namely that the supply is made:-

a) at a time when the premises are open to the members for
   consumption on the premises
b) in a sealed container
c) to a member in person

A separate and distinct Premises Licence may be required in addition to a Club Premises Certificate if a club wishes to sell alcohol to a guest for consumption off the premises, or alcohol is to be sold or supplied to persons other than members or guests for consumption on the premises.

The same will apply if regulated entertainment is to be provided by the club but not to members or guests. This is likely if the club lets rooms for private functions where those attending are not guests under the club rules. In such a case the sale or supply of alcohol will either have to be under a Premises Licence with the authority of a Personal Licence holder and with a Designated Premises Supervisor or under a Temporary Event Notice (see chapter 8).

This could seriously undermine the status of many registered clubs who under the old system were able to let out their premises or part of them for private functions. Unless these clubs change their rules to classify visiting sporting teams and those attending pre-booked functions as guests of the club they will require a Premises Licence with a DPS who holds a Personal Licence.

In the interim review of June 2006 the government made it clear that the Act does not prevent visitors to a qualifying club being supplied with alcohol as long as they are "guests" of any member of the club or the club collectively. "Guest" is not defined by the Act. It is vital that all clubs check their rules and if necessary make amendments. For example they could classify visiting teams and their supporters as "guests".

Club Premises Certificate
To obtain a Club Premises Certificate the club must be a qualifying club for each of the qualifying club activities. A club is a qualifying club for the supply of alcohol to members or guests if it satisfies the general and additional conditions and for provision of regulated entertainment if it satisfies the general conditions.

General Conditions
1. Under the club rules a person may not become a member or enjoy the privileges of membership and members may not enjoy the privileges of membership without an interval of at least two days between their membership application and admission to the club.
2. The club is established and conducted in good faith as a club.
3. The club has at least 25 members.
4. That alcohol is not supplied to members on the premises otherwise than by or on behalf of the club.
5. When establishing whether the club is established and conducted in good faith the licensing authority will consider:-
   a) any arrangements restricting the club's freedom of purchase of alcohol
   b) any provision or arrangement for money or property of the club or gain from club activities to be applied otherwise for the benefit of the club as a whole or for charitable, benevolent or political purposes
6. The arrangement for giving members information about the finances of the club.
7. The books and accounts and other records.
8. The nature of the club's premises.

These are the only matters for consideration set out in the Act.

There is no requirement under the Act for guests to be signed in, but it is advisable to have some record to prove the status of those non-members of the club attending the premises for licensable activities.

The revised guidance of June 2006 suggests that if the club were found to be providing commercial services to the general public it could be contrary to its qualifying club status, but it is difficult to see how this is relevant to the matters listed as criteria for the licensing authority to consider.

Additional Conditions

If not managed by the club in general meeting or by the general body of members, the purchase of alcohol and the supply of alcohol by the club must be managed by a committee of members each 18 years of age or over and elected by the members of the club.

No arrangements must be made for any person to receive at the club's expense any commission on purchases of alcohol by the club. Nor must any arrangements be made for any person to gain by the supply of alcohol to members or guests apart from any benefit of the club as a whole.

There are special savings provisions for industrial and provident societies, friendly societies, and miners' welfare institutes. If a club does not qualify for a Club Premises Certificate it will have to apply for a Premises Licence if it is to carry out a licensable activity.

Procedure

Application for a club premises certificate is made to the licensing authority for the place where the premises are situated. An application must include:-

> ‣ the proper form
> ‣ a plan complying with the regulations
> ‣ the fee
> ‣ a copy of the club rules

The application form includes a club operating schedule, which must detail the qualifying club activities; the times when they are to take place; any other times when the club premises are to be open to members and their guests; whether alcohol is to be supplied and whether for consumption on or off the premises; and what steps are being proposed to meet the four licensing objectives. It is strongly recommended that the club consults all responsible authorities prior to making an application and also considers the advice and model conditions set out in the Guidance itself and its annexes.

A copy of the application form and accompanying documents must also be served on the responsible authorities on the same day as the originals are served on the licensing authority. For a description of responsible authorities, see chapter 3.

Display

The application must be advertised in the proper form by display and newspaper advertisement. Regulations specify the size, colour and contents of the notice as well as print size, font and where it must be placed.

The notice must be displayed for 28 working days starting on the day after the licensing authority receive the notice of application. It should be in a place where the notice can be conveniently read by passers-by without the need for them to enter the property, such as a gate post, or inside a window if that window looks immediately on to the highway.

With large premises (more than 50 square metres) notices must be displayed every 50 metres along the external perimeter abutting any highway. The advertisement must appear in a local newspaper not more than ten working days after the notice of application was given to the licensing authority. It is good practice to send a copy of the advert to the licensing authority without delay.

Plans

Plans must be to a scale of 1:100 on the metric scale (scale endorsed on the plan) unless the licensing authority has agreed in writing beforehand an alternative scale. They must contain the following detail and information - if convenient by way of symbols and colouring with a legend.

a) the extent of the boundary of the building and external and internal walls

b) the perimeter of the premises, to include gardens and grounds used for licensable activities

c) entries, exits and escape routes

d) areas used for each activity where there is more than one licensable activity
e) fixed structures and objects including fixed furniture which may impede emergency evacuation
f) the location and height of any stage or raised areas
g) the location of steps, stairs, elevators and lifts
h) the location of rooms containing public conveniences
i) the location of fire safety equipment, including fire extinguishers, fire doors, emergency lighting and fire alarms
j) any kitchen

Fees

The fee for applications for new Club Premises Certificates is based on the non-domestic rateable value (NDRV) of the premises. There is also an annual fee to be paid based on the NDRV. The formula is:-

NDRV bands
A: £0 to £4,300   B: £4,301 to £33,000
C: £33,001 to £87,000   D: £87,001 to £125,000
E: £125,001 and above

Fees

Bands	A	B	C	D	E
Main Application Fee	100	190	315	450	635
Main Annual Charge	70	180	295	320	350

There are exemptions from fees for clubs whose premises form part of a church hall, parish hall, community hall or similar building and who provide only regulated entertainment. If these clubs supply alcohol, fees will be payable.

On receipt of an application complying with the regulations the authority must, subject to relevant representations, grant the certificate in accordance with the application subject only to conditions consistent with the club operating schedule, including those offered by the club, and any mandatory conditions relating to door supervision. For a description of relevant representations see chapter 3. Such representations must be made within 28 consecutive days starting the day after the application was given to the licensing authority. The representations must concern the likely effect granting the certificate will have on the promotion of the four licensing objectives, ie the prevention of crime and disorder; the interest of public safety; the prevention of public nuisance; and the protection of children from harm.

Where such representations are made the licensing authority must hold a hearing within 20 working days of the end of the time limit for representations unless the authority, the applicant, and each person making a representation considers a hearing unnecessary. The government has issued guidance for interested parties wishing to make representations. This can be found on the DCMS website at http://www.culture .gov.uk/NR/rdonlyres/9F1334B2-09E7-44D7-AE74-D00618EF5F02/0/Guidancemakingrepresentations.pdf.

Where relevant representations are made, the licensing authority in determining the application must take one of three steps which it considers necessary to achieve the licensing objectives namely:-

- ▶ grant the application as made
- ▶ grant the certificate subject to conditions consistent with the club operating schedule modified to meet the licensing objectives
- ▶ exclude from the certificate any of the qualifying club activities
- ▶ reject the application

Door supervision
Where a Club Premises Certificate includes a condition that at specified times there must be security personnel in attendance, the certificate must include a condition that each such individual must be licensed by the Security Industry Authority.

Duration, Changes, Review & Withdrawal of Certificate
Duration: A certificate has effect until it is surrendered or withdrawn.
Surrender: As soon as a club gives notice of surrender and hands the certificate to the licensing authority the certificate lapses.
Withdrawal: The licensing authority must give notice of withdrawal to the club if, in relation to a qualifying club activity, it no longer satisfies qualifying club conditions. The withdrawal may relate to one or more activities.

Review: An interested party, responsible authority or a member of the club may apply for a review of the certificate. There is a procedure for notification, hearing, and determination. The licensing authority must take steps it considers necessary to promote the licensing objectives. This may involve modification of the conditions of the certificate, the exclusion of a qualifying club activity, suspension of the certificate for a period up to three months, or the withdrawal of the certificate.

Determination will not take effect until the end of the 21 day period given for appeal or, if an appeal is made, until it has been disposed of.

For general advice to all stakeholders on best practice in order to avoid the need for review or if necessary how to prepare for that event, refer to chapter 3.

To coincide with the introduction of the Licensing Act the government issued several informal guidances - informal to the extent that they themselves do not have statutory effect. They include one to interested parties applying for a review. This can be accessed on the DCMS website at http://www.culture.gov.uk/NR/rdonlyres/A2DBCE6D -CC18-40DD-A2E7315940A4A599/0/GuidanceReviews.pdf.

Variation

There is provision for application by the club for variation of the Club Premises Certificate. Variation can include any structural alteration to the premises, however small.

It is recommended that the licensing authority be consulted to identify whether a formal variation application is required. The procedure is similar to an application for a new certificate where representations are made. The fees are calculated in the same way as an application for a new certificate. Beware that on application for variation, an authority may if appropriate restrict a certificate rather than extend it in any way.

Change of name, club rules, registered address

The secretary of a club which holds or has made application for a Club Premises Certificate must give notice to the licensing authority of any changes to its name, the club rules, or registered address, and at the same time submit any Club Premises Certificate for amendment. A fee of £10.50 is payable for each notification. The secretary commits an offence if he fails to notify any changes within 28 days of the change. He becomes personally liable to prosecution and a fine of up to of £500.

Fees

Regulations detail fees for application and annual fees for Club Premises Certificates and impose personal liability on the secretary or other officers of the club for payment of those fees.

Keeping and Producing Certificate

The club secretary must give in writing to the authority the name of the person who will keep the Club Premises Certificate or certified copy at the premises. The person should be the secretary, a member of the club, or a person who works at the club premises. He/she must make sure that a summary of the certificates or certified copy of that summary and a notice specifying the position which he/she holds at the premises are permanently displayed at the premises.

A sample notice can be found below. Any copy of the original premises certificate or summary must be certified by the licensing authority, a solicitor or a notary. The nominated person must also provide the Club Premises Certificate or certified copy for examination to a constable or authorised person. Failure to do any of these things is an offence for which the secretary or nominated person may be liable to a fine of up to £500.

[   ]
Licensing Act 2003 - Section 94(4)

I [   ] being the secretary of [   ]
give notice that [   ] of [   ] who works
at the premises for the club and/holds the position of [   ]
[who is a member of the club] is the person nominated to have custody or control at the club premises of the Club Premises Certificate and Summary or certified copies of those documents.

Date: ....…..

Signed: ....
Secretary

41

5

DISCRETIONARY CONDITIONS ON PREMISES LICENCES AND CLUB PREMISES CERTIFICATES

There are two types of condition which can be imposed. Discretionary conditions are detailed here. The second type of condition which can be imposed are mandatory conditions. These are dealt with elsewhere in the chapters on Premises Licences and Club Premises Certificates.

Discretionary conditions can only be imposed if necessary for the promotion of one of the four licensing objectives. There should be no duplication of duties already imposed by other existing legislation.

Hours of Trading

The Guidance recommends that shops, stores and supermarkets selling alcohol should be allowed to sell alcohol during their normal trading hours unless there are exceptional reasons such as problems over disorderly conduct or disturbance.

On premises where the sale and consumption of intoxicating liquor takes place, the Guidance recommends longer opening hours to achieve a slower dispersal of people.

The Guidance makes it clear that licensing authorities should not fix predetermined closing times for areas. In other words they should not zone licensing hours nor should they stagger closing times among premises. In each case the licensing authority should consider the potential for nuisance and what preventative measures might be taken. It should only restrict the hours of trading as a last resort.

It is important that Premises Licences take into account, through their operating schedules, any requirement for extended hours for what used to be referred to as special occasions, such as balls, birthdays, anniversaries, wedding receptions and the like.

Possible occasions for special hours are also Christmas Eve and Day, Boxing Day, Bank Holiday weekends, St George's Day, St Andrew's

Day and St. David's Day. The hours for these extended occasions, identifying hours for each separate licensable activity, and the hours of opening of the premises, must be set out in the operating schedule, which will accompany an application for a Premises Licence or Club Premises Certificate.

General

The Guidance makes it clear that the licensing authority should not impose conditions unless there have been relevant representations which have been considered at a hearing and the authority has determined that conditions are necessary to promote the licensing objectives.

However, it is expected that many applicants for licences will set out their own which they will voluntarily accept. These conditions should become clear on an initial risk assessment after a desirable full consultation with the relevant authorities such as police, fire and environmental health officers. These conditions will be set out in the applicant's operating schedule.

The Guidance stresses that conditions should not be imposed which duplicate existing legislation such as the Licensing Act 2003 which regulates drunken and disorderly behaviour and sales to under age people, and legislation covered by the Environmental Protection Act 1990 and the Noise Act 1996. The Disability Discrimination Act 1995 already provides that any person providing a service to the public must ensure that his premises are adapted to enable disabled people to access them, provided that the cost of doing so is reasonable. Physical obstacles that previously made access unreasonably difficult for disabled people has had to be removed or altered to allow easy access.

There are already sufficient laws governing indecency and obscenity, so additional conditions relating to the content of entertainment such as striptease and lap-dancing should not be imposed.

Conditions should be tailored according to the circumstances. There should be no standardised conditions imposed by licensing authorities.

The Guidance contains model conditions covering the prevention of crime and disorder, public safety, theatres and cinemas, and public nuisance (see the Annexes at the end of this book). Each set of conditions stress that the conditions are not to be regarded as standard and should not be automatically imposed in all cases.

Each application should be considered on its merits. At one end of the scale will be a large nightclub venue in a city centre, whilst at the other will be events put on by groups such as charities, church fetes and schools.

The licensing authority must balance, for instance, the need to ensure the physical safety of event goers against the cost to the organisers of conditions which may be unacceptably high. In considering this balance the licensing authority should look at the history of events held previously and take the views of local residents.

Crime and Disorder Conditions

The Guidance declares that the police should have a key role as the main source of advice and that they should develop working relationships with all the key players including the licensing authority, officers, owners, managers and Designated Premises Supervisors, and the Area Child Protection Committee.

The police should be instrumental in advising on such matters as venue drug policy, protocols for door staff, CCTV installations, protection of employees, and the provision of safe transport home. The model conditions (Annex D) cover:-

Text pagers: as a means of communication between the premises and the police.

Door supervisors: Where the provision of door supervisors is a condition of the licence, they must be registered with the Security Industry Authority. Further conditions may be necessary to deal with operational requirements such as numbers, identification and female supervisors.

Other conditions cover: bottle bans; plastic containers and toughened glass; CCTV; open containers taken from the premises; restrictions on drinking area; capacity limits; proof of age cards; crime prevention notices; drinks promotions and signage.

Regard should be taken of risk. A police authority in one area, for example, has required CCTV coverage of dance floors of all premises where regulated entertainment is provided. Clearly this may be relevant to a busy town centre venue but may not be a proportionate condition for a low risk village pub.

A particular favourite is a condition which also relates to the objective which covers the prevention of harm to children. Many police and authorities representing child protection agencies (in some areas the Trading Standards officer) have required conditions imposing training requirements on all staff selling alcohol in order to deal with the problem of sales to those under 18. Some have wanted conditions requiring a policy to be implemented. The following is a condition which has been offered and accepted:-

"Those engaged in selling or supplying alcohol will obtain sight of evidence of age in the form of either a passport, photo driving licence, or PASS accredited proof of age scheme in the following circumstances:-

▶ *where a person appears to be under 18 and is attempting to buy alcohol*

▶ *where a person is on premises used exclusively or primarily for the sale of alcohol and appears to be under 16 and is not accompanied by an adult*

▶ *where a person is on premises between midnight and 5am, open for the supply of alcohol for consumption there, appears to be under 16 and is not accompanied by an adult."*

A possible variation to this theme could be the adoption of either a 'challenge 21' or perhaps 'challenge 25' policy, depending on the premises and perceived risk, raising the threshold of the age perception which triggers the requirement for proof.

Public Safety

The Guidance suggests that applicants and relevant authorities should consider the following publications regarding the physical safety of the people visiting the premises:-

▶ The Model National and Standard Conditions for Places of Public Entertainment and Associated Guidance

▶ The Event Safety Guide

▶ Managing Crowd Safety

▶ 5 steps to Risk Assessments Case Studies

▶ The Guide to Safety at Sports Events

▶ Safety Guidance for Street Arts, Carnival, Processions and Large Scale Performances

The model conditions (Annex E) cover:-

▶ disabled people

- escape routes
- safety checks
- curtains, hangings, decoration and upholstery
- accommodation limits
- fire action notices
- outbreaks of fire
- loss of water (in the fire fighting context)
- access for emergency vehicles
- first aid
- lighting
- temporary electrical installations
- ventilation
- indoor sports entertainment

There should be no duplication of existing legislation but conditions imposed in respect of other legislation may be varied.

Public Nuisance

The Guidance recognises the difficult balancing act faced by licensing authorities. It states "…it is…important that in applying the relevant objectives, licensing authorities and responsible authorities focus on impacts of the licensing activities at the specific premises on people living, working and sleeping in the vicinity that are disproportionate and unreasonable. The issue will mainly concern noise, nuisance, light pollution and possibly noxious smells."

The model conditions (Annex G) cover:-

- hours: conditions may relate either to the opening hours or to the times when certain activities are permitted such as the playing of music or music and entertainment outside
- noise and vibration
- noxious smells
- light pollution

Again it must be emphasised that conditions should not duplicate the provisions of existing legislation such as the Environmental Protection Act 1990 and Noise Act 1996, and the licensing authority should bear in mind the powers contained in the Licensing Act which enable police officers to close down immediately for up to 24 hours premises causing noise nuisance (see chapter 10).

In practice licensing authorities have imposed a variety of conditions in response to representations on nuisance. There has been a marked difference of approach by authorities.

Examples are:-

▶ doors and windows to be closed when regulated entertainment is taking place

▶ outside areas not to be used after, for example, 10pm

▶ soundproofing

▶ air conditioning

▶ noise limiters on amplification with levels to be set in consultation either with the authority's Environmental Protection Team or expert consultant

▶ regular logged perimeter checks on noise

▶ notices displayed at all exits requesting customers to leave quietly

Outside entertainment has provoked the greatest number of complaints. Under the old law private parties at commercial premises required no public entertainment licence and were by and large unregulated. Now that this is included in regulated entertainment we are seeing conditions attached limiting the number of these type of events as well as their hours of operation.

Late night refreshment premises have posed their own set of problems, with complaints about noise, litter and general disturbance. Many have seen their hours of operation (often previously unregulated) cut back and conditions imposed particularly to deal with litter. At least one authority has requiried such premises to provide customers with toilet facilities.

It must be borne in mind that conditions must be proportionate. It may be unreasonable, for instance, to require a small premises or a club with limited resources to install costly soundproofing and air-conditioning.

Children

An applicant may offer, or the licensing authority can impose, conditions which support the licensing objective of protecting children from harm. It is important to remember that the age restrictions do not mean that a premises must admit children who comply. Each premises may have its own policy which may be more restrictive, but not more lenient, than either the law or conditions on the licence.

The relevance of conditions relating to the admission of children to the premises depends entirely on the use being made of the premises. For example children may be excluded altogether when entertainment of an adult nature is occurring, or they may be excluded except between certain hours or admitted only if accompanied by an adult, according to the circumstances.

These discretionary conditions are in addition to the statutory restrictions. As in every application it is important that a risk assessment is undertaken which is specific to the location and intended use of the premises. A known local problem with under age drinking in pubs should trigger more stringent proposals to deal with prevention (see earlier).

Model conditions and discussion are contained in Annex H to the Guidance. They include provision for admission to cinemas and theatres as well as participation of children in performances. For more details see chapter 9.

Small venues and entertainment

The new licensing regime contains complex provisions to exempt some small venues which provide entertainment from the effect of some discretionary conditions which may be attached to their premises licence whilst entertainment is being provided.

The first exemptions apply to premises used primarily for the supply of alcohol for consumption on the premises, eg a pub which also provides musical entertainment which can be amplified or un-amplified.

If the whole of the premises has a permitted capacity of no more than 200, then any discretionary conditions imposed by the licensing authority will have no effect so far as provision of that music entertainment is concerned, unless they relate to the prevention of crime and disorder or public safety. For example, any conditions requiring noise limiters would not apply but those insisting on door staff would. Note that mandatory conditions and those offered by the licensee will still apply.

The second exemption applies to any premises authorised for music entertainment of un-amplified live music. If the premises has a permitted capacity of no more than 200, and the music is played between 8am and midnight, no licensing authority imposed conditions of any description will apply. Examples of this might be where the conditions require door staff for the entertainment or where there is a requirement for doors and windows to remain closed for the entertainment.

But there is a warning. Any nuisance or disturbance, particularly to local residents or businesses, will most likely result in an application for a review of the Premises Licence. On a successful review, the licensing authority has power to order that the suspended conditions will apply, in whole or part, as well as any new conditions which they consider necessary to safeguard any one or more of the four licensing objectives (see chapter 3).

6

PERSONAL LICENCES

Alcohol may only be sold or supplied on premises:-
1. which have a Premises Licence, under the authority of someone who holds a Personal Licence, and when there is a premises supervisor who holds a Personal Licence
2. which have a Club Premises Certificate
3. where the user is the holder of a Temporary Event Notice provided that the alcohol is sold under the authority of that user

In their June 2006 review of the Guidance the government made it clear that a Personal Licence holder need not be personally present at every transaction and it is not necessary for a separate authorisation to be given for each sale of alcohol. This should allow small operators to give written authority to someone managing premises in their absence to sell alcohol, allowing them to go on holiday without the fear, as happened with one pub in Yorkshire, that the police will close down the premises in their absence (they have no power to do this anyway).

The grant of Personal Licences is dealt with by the licensing authority for the area in which the applicant is ordinarily resident. If the applicant is not ordinarily resident in England or Wales the grant of a licence may be dealt with by any licensing authority. Renewals can only be dealt with by the licensing authority which granted the Personal Licence.

An individual may hold only one Personal Licence. Once granted, the licence lasts for ten years unless revoked or surrendered.

Application and grant of licence
Application must be served on the correct licensing authority in accordance with the regulations. The documents which must be served are:-
▶ the proper form
▶ the fee of £37

▶ two photographs 45mm x 35mm taken on photographic paper, full face on light background, no hats or sunglasses worn. One of the photographs must be endorsed as a true likeness by a solicitor, notary, an individual with a professional qualification such as a doctor, accountant or teacher, or a person of standing in the community such as a bank or building society official, civil servant or minister of religion.

▶ A copy of the licensing qualification (NCPLH, GOAL, or GQAL) (see chapter 7)

▶ A Criminal Record Bureau basic disclosure certificate issued no earlier than one month before the application is made. These can be obtained from Disclosure Scotland. www.disclosurescotland.co.uk (allow up to six weeks from payment clearance).

▶ A declaration in the proper form that no relevant or foreign offences have been committed, or if they have, details of them.

The licensing authority must grant the licence if the applicant satisfies all of the following conditions:-

a) he/she is 18 years old or over
b) he/she possesses an accredited licensing qualification awarded by an accredited body (see chapter 7)
c) no Personal Licence held by him/her has been forfeited in the previous five years
d) he/she has not been convicted of any relevant offence or any foreign offence (ie outside England and Wales)

If the applicant fails to comply with a), b) or c) the licensing authority must reject the application.

If the applicant satisfies the first three conditions but fails to satisfy d), the licensing authority must give the police notice. The police then have 14 days from receiving the application to decide whether in the light of a relevant offence the granting of a Personal Licence would undermine the crime prevention objective. In the case of a foreign offence they will consider whether the offence is comparable to a relevant offence.

If the police fail to give notice of objection within the 14 days the licensing authority must grant the application. If the police do object, the licensing authority must hold a hearing within 20 working days of the end of the 14 day period to consider the police objection.

They must reject the application if they consider it necessary for the promotion of the crime prevention objective. The Guidance recommends refusal unless there are "exceptional and compelling" circumstances.

Relevant Offence

Convictions for a relevant offence must be disregarded if they are spent under the Rehabilitation of Offenders Act 1974. Life imprisonment is excluded. Other offences have a rehabilitation period of between five and ten years. Otherwise the following are relevant offences:-

▶ where a custodial sentence has been imposed of at least 30 months for:-

a) certain sexual offences

b) violence namely one which leads, is intended to lead or likely to lead to death or physical injury

c) certain offences under the Theft Acts including those of theft, robbery, burglary, aggravated burglary and obtaining services by deception

d) offences under the Forgery and Counterfeiting Act 1981 other than those of reproducing British currency notes or making imitation British coins

▶ an offence under the Licensing Act 2003

▶ an offence under various licensing acts

▶ an offence under the Firearms Act 1968 and amendment acts of 1988 and 1997

▶ allowing a child to take part in gaming on premises licensed for the sale of alcohol

▶ certain offences under the Misuse of Drugs Act 1971

▶ certain offences under the Customs and Excise Management Act 1979

▶ certain offences under the Tobacco Products Duty Act 1979

▶ certain offences under the Road Traffic Act 1988 namely causing death by careless driving while under the influence of drink or drugs, driving when under such influence, or driving with excess alcohol

▶ An offence of engaging in security activities in contravention of the Private Security Industry Act 2001

Renewal

Application to renew is made to the licensing authority which granted the licence. If since the grant - but in the case of a later renewal since that renewal - the applicant has been convicted of any relevant or foreign offence, the licensing authority must give notice to the police.

If the police believe that renewing the licence would undermine the crime prevention objective they must give notice to the licensing authority within 14 days. If the police do so a hearing must be held to consider the objection. The licensing authority must grant the application if the police fail to give notice or if after a hearing it does not consider it necessary to reject the application in the interests of crime prevention.

The fee for renewal is the same as for the original grant, currently £37.

Convictions during application period

If during the period between the application having been made and its determination or withdrawal the applicant is convicted of a relevant or foreign offence he must as soon as reasonably practicable notify the licensing authority. Failure to do so without reasonable excuse is an offence subject to a maximum fine of £2,500.

Convictions coming to light after grant or renewal

If after grant or renewal the licensing authority becomes aware of a conviction during the application period for a relevant offence it must give notice to the police.

If the police consider that continuation of the licence would undermine the licensing objective it must give an objection notice, a hearing must take place, and the licensing authority must revoke the licence if it considers that otherwise it would undermine the crime prevention objective.

Licence Holder's Duties

▶ To produce the licence to a constable or authorised officer where the holder is on premises to make or authorise the supply of alcohol under a Premises Licence or Temporary Event Notice. If the licence has been lost, stolen, damaged or destroyed a copy can be obtained from the licensing authority on payment of the fee of £10.50. If the licence has been lost or stolen the holder must first report the loss or theft to the police.

▶ To notify change of name or address as soon as reasonably practicable. A fee of £10.50 is payable.

▶ To produce the Personal Licence to the court no later than first appearance where charged with a relevant offence or at first appearance before conviction and sentencing or acquittal following the grant of a licence. If after production and before conviction and sentencing, or acquittal, the holder makes or withdraws an application for renewal, or the renewal takes place, or the licence is surrendered or revoked, the holder must notify the court at the next court appearance.

▶ To notify the licensing authority of conviction of a foreign offence.

▶ To notify the licensing authority of conviction of a relevant offence where the convicting court has not been notified of the Personal Licence, or is not aware of it. This does not apply in the limited offences listed earlier for which a custodial sentence of less than 30 months has been imposed

Failure to notify or produce in respect of any of the above duties is an offence subject to a maximum fine of £500.

Sentencing Court's Powers

Where the holder of a Personal Licence is convicted of a relevant offence the court may order the forfeiture of the licence or order its suspension for a period not exceeding six months. The court and any appeal court has power to suspend such an order.

Where the court has convicted a licence holder of a relevant offence it must notify the licence authority of the details of the Personal Licence and of the conviction and sentence. It must also send a copy to the licence holder.

It does not have to give notice where the offence was one of the limited offences listed earlier where a custodial sentence of at least 30 months was not imposed, unless the court made an order for forfeiture or suspension of the Personal Licence.

7

TRAINING & QUALIFICATIONS

The combination of the Licensing Act 2003 and the Private Security Industry Act 2001 require necessary qualifications in two areas relating to licensed premises - Personal Licences and door supervision.

Apart from the main qualifications listed below, there are many other qualifications available which are recommended for staff working in the alcohol and entertainment industry. The BIIAB Level 1 Award in Responsible Alcohol Retailing, for instance, targets bar staff, waiters and waitresses, supermarket cashiers, and licensed shop cashiers. More information can be obtained from the BIIAB website: www.biiab.org.

Personal Licences

The licensing authority must reject an application for a Personal Licence if the applicant does not have the necessary licensing qualification or is not a person of a prescribed description (yet to be prescribed at the time of publication).

The licensing qualification must be accredited by the Secretary of State and awarded by a body also accredited, or an equivalent qualification awarded in Scotland, Northern Ireland or other European Economic Area member (not the UK).

The syllabus published by the Government includes the following subjects:-

▸ Licensing Authorities
▸ Licensable Activities
▸ Alcohol
▸ Personal Licences
▸ Premises Licences
▸ Permitted Temporary Activities
▸ Operating Schedules

▶ Police Powers
▶ Disorderly Conduct
▶ Protection of Children
▶ Rights of Entry

The holder of a Personal Licence can operate in any type of premises which hold a Premises Licence and the qualification covers the full range of licensing.

At present there are just three awarding bodies:

1. British Institute of Innkeeping (BII): Level 2 National Certificate for Personal Licence Holders. Contact telephone 01276 684449; website www.bii.org; email qualifications@bii.org.

2. Education Development International (EDI): GOAL Level 2 Certificate for Personal Licence Holders. Contact telephone 08707 202909; website www.ediplc.com; email customerservice@ediplc.com.

3. The Pubshop Ltd: GQ AL National Certificate for Personal Licence Holders. Contact telephone 01305 786 639; website www.nationaltrainingco.com; email enquiries@pubshop.co.uk

Personal Licences are not required for premises which operate under a Club Premises Certificate.

Anyone buying or leasing premises which hold a Premises Licence for the sale of alcohol should make sure that there is someone with a Personal Licence who can take on the role of Designated Premises Supervisor.

It is not be possible to take over premises and then obtain the necessary qualifications, as was possible under the old system of licensing. It is important to obtain the necessary qualifications well in advance of any application for a Personal Licence.

Door Supervisors

Anyone who wishes to work as a door supervisor on licensed premises open to the public needs a licence from the Security Industry Authority (SIA). This includes employers and managers of door supervisors but not, for example, pub landlords who receive the services under contract but who have some supervisory responsibility, and not premises which have a Club Premises Certificate.

Potential holders of a licence must obtain the approved training and qualification and satisfy the SIA that he/she is a suitable candidate. In particular criminal record checks are undertaken. Convictions or cautions are considered in accordance with their relevance, seriousness, and how recent they were. In the event of registration refusal an appeal can be made to the magistrates' court.

The new licensing system has operated countrywide since April 2005. For further information see the SIA website www.the-sia.org.uk.

Applications can be made to the SIA by telephone (08702 430 100) or on-line at the website address given above. The fee for the three year period of the licence is £190.

The qualification is awarded on successful completion of 28 hours' training including two examinations following each of two 14 hour training sessions. The first training session covers the role and responsibilities of a door supervisor and the second on communication skills and conflict management. There are a number of approved awarding bodies who will each have their own approved course providers.

Door supervisors who have already completed training courses and hold qualifications may be exempt from obtaining the new qualifications. For a list of exemptions and more information visit the SIA website www.the-sia.org.uk/licences/doors-previous-qualifications.asp.

8

PERMITTED TEMPORARY ACTIVITIES

If an event involving a licensable activity is planned to take place on premises which do not have a Premises Licence or Club Premises Certificate, or which do have one but not for the intended licensable activity or hours required, the organiser must give a Temporary Event Notice (TEN).

TENs can only be given by a named individual. This can be for a one-off event such as a dance in an unlicensed village hall or it could be on behalf of holders of Premises Licences and Club Premises Certificates who wish to hold events which may go beyond their licence or certificate conditions, either in terms of licensable activities, hours of operation or other restrictions. So, for example, whilst New Year's Eve is automatically covered by an extension of licensing hours from 11pm that night, other holidays such as Christmas Eve and Bank Holidays are not covered and a holder may wish such a holiday to be covered.

Premises include not just buildings or parts of buildings but outside areas such as parks recreation areas temporary structures such as marquees and private land.

If extensions are required then TENs must be given but beware the limits set out below. It may be necessary and cheaper to apply for a variation of the Premise Licence or Club Premises Certificate. Where major variations are required an entirely new licence or certificate may be preferable.

The restrictions are:-

a) The event must last no longer than 96 hours

b) Individual premises must not be the subject of TENS exceeding a total of 15 days per calendar year

c) The number of people on the premises at any one time must not exceed 499 including staff, organisers, stewards and performers

d) A holder of a Personal Licence including an associate can give no more than 50 TENs per calendar year

e) Premises cannot be used for a TEN more than 12 times per calendar year

f) Someone who is not the holder of a Personal Licence including an associate can give no more than five TENs per calendar year

g) Holders of Club Premises Certificates are unusually restricted. Unless the individual applying holds a Personal Licence the applicant will be limited to just five TENs per calendar year.

If these limits are exceeded the licensing authority will serve a counter notice on the applicant and the police. There is no right of appeal.

Procedure

Two copies of the notice must be given to the licensing authority for the area where the event is to take place, and one copy to the police for that area, at least ten working days before the proposed licensable activity or activities are to begin.

The applicant must be an individual who must be aged 18 or over. The notice must be in the proper form and accompanied by the fee of £21.

The licensing authority must acknowledge receipt within two working days. This should take the form of the signature of a person authorised to acknowledge receipt on the notice itself or a copy of it. If the limits have been exceeded (see above) a counter notice will be served.

From receipt of notice the police only have 48 hours in which to object. If objecting, they must give notice to the authority and applicant. They can serve notice of objection either by delivery in person, leaving it at the correct address, sending it to the correct address by ordinary post, or by sending it by email to an email address provided in the notice.

The authority must then hold a hearing within seven days of the end of the 48 hour period. The police objection must be that the event would undermine the crime prevention objective, and if the authority agrees it must give the applicant a counter notice, which would mean that the event must not take place.

This whole process must be completed at least 24 hours before the proposed start time of the planned event. Because of the timescale of the procedure it is advisable, particularly for major events, that the TEN is served well in advance, and after consultation with the police and authority. Advance planning consultation and co-operation will be the key to successful events.

Obligations

1. To give access to the premises at any reasonable time to an authorised officer or police constable
2. To prominently display a copy of the TEN or keep it at the premises in the possession of the applicant or nominated person present and working at the premises and to display a notice identifying that person
3. To produce the TEN to a police constable on request

Failure to comply is an offence carrying a maximum fine of £500. The holder of a TEN must be aware of the offences under the Licensing Act which could apply to him or her, including those relating to the sale and supply of alcohol to under persons under 18, unsupervised sale of alcohol by persons under 18, admission of children to premises particularly where alcohol is being consumed, allowing disorderly behaviour, and the sale of alcohol to those who are already drunk (see chapters 9 and 10).

All TENS are subject to a mandatory condition where alcohol is supplied that all supplies must be made by or under the authority of the named premises user who is of course the individual applicant.

Breach could result in the prosecution of both the holder of the TEN and the person making the supply. It is recommended that the holder gives prior written authority to all staff involved in supplying alcohol at the event and should keep safely copies signed by the relevant staff.

9

CHILDREN

Societies rarely tolerate lawful supply of alcohol to children and often restrict their access to premises where alcohol is consumed. The Licensing Act 2003 only tinkers with the restrictions in place for much of the last century. However, it recognises that the protection of children from harm is a central issue and makes it one of the four licensing objectives which guide every licensing decision.

There are provisions which, on the one hand, give discretion and flexibility to the licensing authority and on the other provide heavy sanctions for law breakers. Unless the authority has placed a condition restricting their presence during certain licensable activities in terms of times or during certain licensable activities, accompanied children under 16 years old are allowed on licensed premises.

Children on Licensed Premises

Where premises are used exclusively or primarily for alcohol sale and consumption, or are open for a permitted activity with a Temporary Event Notice, children under 16 years are not allowed on premises when they are open for the sale and consumption of alcohol, unless accompanied by an adult. This also applies to anyone under 16 employed on the premises. No doubt they will usually be accompanied by an adult.

There is no restriction on premises which sell or supply alcohol for consumption off the premises. Entertainment venues such as nightclubs, sporting venues, cinemas, many members' clubs, and other premises not used exclusively or mainly for the sale and consumption of alcohol, are not restricted in this way, save that children under 16 must be accompanied by an adult between the hours of midnight and 5am.

However, the licensing authority may impose conditions which restrict or prevent access altogether, if to do so would satisfy one or more of the licensing objectives, such as the protection of children from harm. Adult entertainment venues are restricted in this way. Venues can of course set their own rules for admission, restricting access beyond the statutory provisions if they wish to do so. Allowing an unaccompanied child under 16 years on relevant premises is an offence. Anyone working on the premises with authority to exclude them, or the holder of the Premises Licence, the Designated Premises Supervisor, or a member or officer of a club, or the user of a Temporary Event Notice may be convicted and fined up to £1,000.

Premises converted from a Justices On Licence under the transitional provisions remain subject to the provisions of the old law set out in the Licensing Act 1964 unless they applied for a variation to remove the old legal restrictions. As a result some premises could still be subject to the 'no under 14s in a bar' rule, unless the premises had a Childrens' Certificate for that area.

It is difficult for customers to discover the restrictions before entering premises. Under 16s have to be accompanied by an adult in the circumstances described earlier but, where the old law carries over, under 14s may still be excluded from bar areas even when accompanied by an adult. A premises operator wishing to welcome those under 14 will in those circumstances have to apply for a variation of the Premises Licence to allow under 14s in bar areas.

Purchase and Consumption of Alcohol

Someone under 18 years old cannot hold a Personal Licence; a Premises Licence; or Temporary Event Notice. A person under 18 years old commits an offence if he breaches these restrictions.

Neither may a person under 18 buy or attempt to buy alcohol or acquire alcohol from the club if he/she is a member of it.

A person under 18 may not consume alcohol on licensed premises, premises with a Club Premises Certificate or premises used for a permitted temporary activity. No offence is committed if the person is aged 16 or 17 and the alcohol is beer, wine or cider, consumed at a table with a meal, and the individual is accompanied by someone aged 18 or over.

The Licensing Act 2003 is more punitive and restrictive than previous legislation. For instance the old law made it an offence for someone under 18 to consume alcohol in a bar of licensed premises, but not in a restaurant or restaurant area. The offence is now committed in all areas of premises licensed for the sale of alcohol.

Sale, Supply and Acquisition of Alcohol

A person commits an offence if:-

a) he/she sells alcohol to an individual aged under 18

b) he/she supplies alcohol on behalf of a club to or for a member aged under 18 or for a person under 18 whether or not that person is a member. (The club also commits an offence in this instance)

c) a worker at the premises with authority to prevent a sale knowingly allows the sale of alcohol to an individual under 18 years

d) a worker at club premises with authority or a member or officer of a club present at the premises, in a capacity to prevent a supply, knowingly allows alcohol to be supplied to or for a member or anyone under 18 years old whether or not that person is a member

e) he/she buys or acquires or attempts to buy or acquire alcohol for someone aged under 18. There is an exception where the buyer is 18 years old and the person for whom the alcohol is purchased is 16 or 17, and where the alcohol is beer, wine or cider, and its purchase or supply is for consumption by the 16 or 17 year old at a table and with a meal.

Although breaches of a) and b) are offences, any person charged will have a defence if he can prove that he believed the individual was 18 years old or over and either all reasonable steps had been taken to establish their age or no-one could reasonably have suggested from the person's appearance that they were under 18 years.

Reasonable steps means asking for evidence and the evidence being sufficient to convince a reasonable person. Where a person is accused because of the conduct of someone else, that person has a defence that the/she exercised "all due diligence" to avoid the offence. This is where thorough staff training, the adoption of a rigorous challenge policy and the retention of records, is vital.

There are similar offences relating to the sale or supply of liqueur confectionery to children under 16.

Delivery, Go-betweens and Unsupervised Sales

A person commits an offence if:-

1. whilst working on licensed premises he knowingly delivers to someone under 18 years old alcohol, sold or supplied on the premises,

by or on behalf of a club to or on the instructions of a club member

2. whilst working on licensed premises with the authority to prevent delivery, knowingly allows anybody else to deliver alcohol which has been sold on the licensed premises to someone aged under 18

3. whilst working on licensed premises with the authority to prevent the supply, or being a member or officer of the club on the premises at the time with the capacity to prevent supply, knowingly allows anyone else to deliver to someone under 18 years alcohol supplied on the licensed premises by or on behalf of a club on the instructions of a club member

4. he knowingly sends an individual aged under 18 to obtain alcohol sold on the premises for consumption off the premises or alcohol supplied by a club to or on the instructions of a member for consumption off the premises. (No offence is committed where the person under 18 works on the premises in a capacity which involves the delivery of alcohol)

5. being either the holder of the Premises Licence, Designated Premises Supervisor, or premises user for a permitted temporary activity, or someone aged 18 or over duly authorised by such a person, or on club premises a member or officer present, or responsible person having the capacity to prevent supply, knowingly allows someone under 18 to sell alcohol on licensed premises or supply alcohol by or on behalf of the club to a member. This does not apply if the sale or supply has been specifically approved by such responsible persons. Neither is it an offence for anyone under 18 to sell or deliver alcohol for consumption with a table meal in an area reserved for diners, so this will allow waiters and waitresses under 18 to serve alcohol to diners.

The first three situations are not offences if the alcohol is delivered at a place where the buyer or person supplied lives or works, or the individual under 18 works on the premises involving delivery of alcohol, or the alcohol is sold or supplied for consumption on the licensed premises.

Enforcement

A wide range of powers and penalties are available to the police and other authorities. These include Anti-Social Behaviour Orders, Fixed Penalty Notices, and closure of premises where offences are committed.

10

OFFENCES, CLOSURE OF PREMISES, RIGHTS OF ENTRY AND NOISE

Offences

The Licensing Act 2003 is awash with criminal offences which may catch the unwary. The following list is not exhaustive and is by no means in order of severity.

1. The holder of a Premises Licence must notify the relevant licensing authority of any change in his name or address or that of the Designated Premises Supervisor. The maximum fine is currently £500.

2. The licence holder must notify the Designated Premises Supervisor of any change or rejection of change of the Designated Premises Supervisor. The maximum fine is currently £1,000.

3. Within 14 days of service of notice of a change of Designated Premises Supervisor, the licence holder must send to the licensing authority the Premises Licence or a statement why it is not practicable to do so. The maximum fine is currently £1,000.

4. Children: See chapter 9. Fines range from £2,000 to £5,000.

5. A person commits an offence if he knowingly or recklessly makes a false statement in connection with an application for the grant, variation, transfer or review of a Premises Licence or Club Premises Certificate, an application for a Provisional Statement, a Temporary Event Notice, or interim authority notice or any other notice under the Act, an application for the grant or renewal of a Personal Licence, or a notice by a freeholder conferring the right to be notified of changes to the licensing register. The maximum fine is currently £5,000.

6. Offences relating to closure orders and rights of entry: see the relevant section later.

7. A person may not carry on or knowingly allow an unauthorised licensable activity. There are exceptions for those whose only involvement is participation in a performance or event. The maximum penalty

is six months' imprisonment, a fine of £20,000, or both. There is a defence of due diligence.

8. The retail selling of alcohol as an unauthorised licensable activity carries a maximum penalty of six months imprisonment, a fine of £20,000, or both. There is a defence of due diligence.

9. Keeping alcohol on premises for unauthorised sale carries a maximum penalty of £500. There is a defence of due diligence.

10. Allowing disorderly conduct on licensed premises attracts a maximum penalty of £1,000. It applies to the relevant holder of a Premises Licence, Designated Premises Supervisor, member or officer of a club present with the capacity to prevent it, the premises user under a permitted temporary activity, and any person who works on the premises having authority to prevent such conduct.

11. Sale of alcohol to a person who is drunk or allowing such a sale carries a maximum penalty of £1,000. It applies to those persons mentioned under item 10 above.

12. Any person who knowingly obtains, for a person who is drunk on licensed premises, alcohol for consumption there commits an offence for which the maximum penalty is £1,000.

13. A person who is drunk or disorderly commits an offence if without reasonable excuse he fails to leave the licensed premises or attempts to enter or enters such premises when requested not to. A request can be made by a constable, a person working at the premises with authority to make the request, a Premises Licence holder, or a Designated Premises Supervisor, a club member or officer, licensing authority, or the premises user under a Temporary Event Notice. The maximum penalty is £200.

14. The secretary of a club which holds a Premises Certificate or has made application for one, must notify the licensing authority of any change in the name or alteration of the rules of the club within 28 days. The maximum penalty is £500.

15. The secretary of a club which holds a Premises Certificate and which ceases to have authority to use its registered address must notify the licensing authority of the change as soon as reasonably practical. The maximum penalty is £500.

16. The secretary of a club holding a Premises Certificate must produce the certificate to the licensing authority within 14 days of a request. The maximum penalty for non-compliance is £500.

17. The secretary of a club holding a Premises Certificate must ensure that it or a certified copy is kept at the premises in the custody of a person who has been identified by notice to the licensing authority. The person may be the secretary, any member of the club, or someone who works at the premises. Failure to do so risks a maximum penalty of £500. The nominated person must also ensure that the summary of the certificate or certified copy of the summary and a notice of the position he holds are prominently displayed at the premises. Failure to do so attracts a similar penalty, as does failure to produce the certificate to a police-constable or authorised person.

Proceedings for offences under the Act may be instituted by the licensing authority, the Director of Public Prosecutions, or in case of sale of alcohol to children by the local weights and measures authority.

Closure of Premises

The police can request a closure of the premises for up to 24 hours where there is or expected to be disorder. These powers only apply to premises with a Premises Licence or subject to a Temporary Event Notice. They do not apply to a club operating solely under a Club Premises Certificate.

The magistrates for the area can order the closure for up to 24 hours of all premises having a Premises Licence or Temporary Event Notice in the area of disorder or expected disorder. An order may only be made on the application of a police officer of the rank of superintendent or above and only if the court is satisfied that it is necessary to prevent disorder. Failure to comply carries a maximum penalty of £1,000.

A police officer of the rank of inspector or above, may make a Closure Order for identified premises holding a Premises Licence or Temporary Event Notice if he reasonably believes that there is or is likely imminently to be disorder on or in the vicinity of and related to the premises. The closure must be necessary in the interests of public safety, or to prevent a public nuisance being caused by noise coming from the premises.

A Closure Order by the police comes into force immediately notice of it is received by the holder of the Premises Licence, Designated Premises Supervisor, premises under a Temporary Event Notice, or the manager of the premises. The closure will be for a specified period up to a maximum of 24 hours. An offence is committed if, without reasonable excuse, a person permits premises to be open in contravention of the order. The maximum penalty is three months' imprisonment, a fine of £20,000, or both.

The officer who made the order or another designated officer holding the rank of inspector or above must as soon as reasonably practicable apply to the magistrates' court to consider the order, and any extension of it, and notify the licensing authority. A closure can be extended by the police for a further 24 hours where the conditions for closure remain and the magistrates are unlikely to consider the original order before it expires.

On hearing the application the court may revoke a Closure Order, order the premises to remain closed until the licensing authority has reviewed the Premises Licence, or allow exceptional opening or opening subject to conditions. A person allowing opening in contravention of a court's Closure Order is liable to a penalty of imprisonment, a fine of up to £20,000, or both.

An appeal against a court order must be made to the Crown Court within 21 days.

It should be noted that the closure provisions do not apply to clubs holding only Club Premises Certificates.

Where a Closure Order has come into effect for identified premises after a police Closure Order the court must notify the licensing authority who must then review the Premises Licence and make a decision within 28 days.

Regulations provide for notice and advertisement of the review with a time limit for representation by the holder of the Premises Licence, interested party (persons living in or involved in business in the vicinity etc) or responsible authority (police, fire authority, planning authority etc). A hearing must be held. On review the licensing authority can modify the conditions of the Premises Licence; exclude a licensable activity; remove the Designated Premises Supervisor; suspend the licence for a period up to three months; or revoke the licence.

Any decision will not take effect until the end of the period allowed for appeals and if an appeal is made until it is disposal of. However, where the decision is not to revoke the licence and the premises have remained closed under a Closure Order, the decision will take effect from the time the holder of the licence is notified.

The police have limited exemption from liability for damages for any act or omission relating to a Closure Order. The exemption does not apply if bad faith is established or if the police action amounts to a breach of the Human Rights Act.

Local authorities also have a power of closure which is exercisable by its chief executive officer through an environmental health officer (EHO). A Closure Order may be made where the EHO reasonably believes that a public nuisance is being caused by noise coming from the premises and closure is necessary to prevent it. It takes effect immediately the manager of the premises receives it and lasts for up to 24 hours.

Failure to comply with the order is a criminal offence carrying a maximum penalty of three months' imprisonment, a fine of up to £20,000, or both.

Rights of Entry

A police constable or an authorised person (officer of the relevant licensing authority, fire officer, public health/environmental pollution officer, health and safety officer) may enter any premises being used for a licensable activity or are intended to be used for such an activity.

Such persons must produce identity on request. They may use reasonable force, if necessary. Anyone intentionally obstructing the right of entry is liable to a fine up to £1,000. The right does not extend to club premises which has a Club Premises Certificate but has no other authorisation such as a Premises Licence or Temporary Event Notice.

A constable may enter and search any premises including those with a Club Premises Certificate if he has reason to believe that an offence under the Licensing Act has been committed, is being or is about to be committed. If necessary reasonable force may be used. For other rights of entry to premises with a Club Premises Certificate see chapter 4.

Fixed Penalty Notices and fines

Since 1st November 2004 the police have had power to give fixed penalty notices not only to those committing anti-social behaviour but also to anyone selling alcohol to under 18s or allowing under 18s to consume alcohol on their premises.

These powers are likely to be extended in the near future to include the power to close premises which have been the subject of a certain number of fixed penalty notices. These powers are in addition to the penalties and closure orders mentioned above.

It is clear that the police and licensing authorities combined have a formidable array of enforcement powers which they are likely to employ particularly in problem areas and premises. These powers have been employed in the campaigns run to date, known as AMECs (Alcohol Misuse Enforcement Campaign), the last of which was launched prior to football's 2006 World Cup.

So-called 'sting' tactics using children are lawfully employed to catch those willing to sell alcohol to anyone under 18 years of age, and those who do not carry out stringent identity checks.

Relevant examples of offences which can attract fixed penalty notices and the penalties themselves are:-

1. sale of alcohol to someone under 18: £80 if offender aged 16 or over; £40 if aged between 10 and 15 years.

2. purchase of alcohol by someone under 18: £80 if offender 16 or over; £40 if aged between 10 and 15 years.

3. purchase of alcohol by someone under 18: £50 if offender aged 16 or over; £30 if aged between 10 and 15 years.

4. delivery of alcohol/allowing delivery to a person under 18: £80 if offender aged 16 or over; £40 if aged between 10 and 15 years.

5. consumption of alcohol/allowing consumption by a person under 18 on premises licensed for the sale of alcohol: £50 if offender aged 16 or over; £30 if between 10 and 15 years.

6. sale of alcohol to a person who is drunk: £80 if offender is aged 16 or over; £40 if aged between 10 and 15 years.

7. consumption of alcohol in designated public place: £50 if offender is aged 16 or over; £30 if aged between 10 and 15 years.

8. disorderly behaviour while drunk in a public place: £80 if the offender is aged 16 or over; £40 if between 10 and 15 years.

9. being drunk in a highway, public place or on licensed premises: £80 if the offender is aged 16 or over; £40 if between 10 and 15 years.

Should someone under 16 years attract a penalty notice, the police may within 28 days of attracting it serve such a notice on the recipient's parent or guardian. The parent or guardian must pay the penalty within the statutory time allowed for payment of all fixed penalty notices which is 21 days.

Fixed penalty notices not paid within 21 days will be registered with a court as a fine and will be enforced by the court. If the notice is disputed a court hearing must be requested within the 21 day period. The court will then issue a summons with a hearing date. If the fine is not paid nor a hearing requested within 21 days, the fine registered will be one and a half times the fixed penalty sum.

It is therefore very important that penalty notices are dealt with quickly either by payment of the fine or challenged by application to the court. This is vital to those working in the trade since the accumulation of fixed penalties could put in danger both Premises Licences and Personal Licences. At least one licensing authority believes that just one fixed penalty notice for the sale of alcohol to under aged persons should result in a review of the Premises Licence concerned.

Noise

In addition to the police powers to close premises due to noise nuisance and the separate powers available to the Environmental Health Authority to close premises, from 1st October 2006 the Noise Act 1996 gives local authorities additional powers to control noise coming from licensed premises including those operating under a Temporary Event Notice.

There is a lower level of enforcement to Closure Orders and Abatement Notices. Previously noise nuisance had to be so serious that it justified a Noise Abatement Notice. The new powers mean that if a local resident complains of excessive noise nuisance between 11pm and 7am the Environmental Health Officer must investigate.

If the officer considers the noise excessive he can issue a formal written warning. Should the noise continue he can issue a fixed penalty notice or take court action against the person responsible. This will usually be the holder of the Premises Licence or Temporary Event Notice but could be a manager or employee left in charge at the time of the nuisance. Fixed penalty fines are expected to be £500 and the maximum fine on any conviction £5,000. It is also likely that in the event of persistent noise nuisance either the local residents or Environmental Health Officer will seek a review of the Premises Licence.

11

APPEALS

Any appeal will usually be to the local magistrates' court unless some unusual point of law requires an application to the High Court for a judicial review. The government has issued guidance notes for interested parties looking to appeal against decisions of the licensing authority. These can be accessed on the DCMS website at www.culture.gov.uk/alcohol_and _entertainment/advice_and_guidance.

The guidance notes are advisory only. They have no force and, in fact, in at least one regard they are incorrect. The notes suggest that a "licensing authority's decision will take effect immediately, until the outcome of any appeal is known". In fact, this is not the case about any decision taken at a review hearing. The Act specifically provides that a decision following an application for review will not have effect until the end of the period for appeal and, where an appeal is made, until it has been disposed of. Some experts believe that the government has in mind a change in the law but its guidance is premature in that respect.

Premises Licence
An applicant for a licence or provisional statement, or interim authority or the holder of a licence, whichever is relevant, may appeal against decisions of the licensing authority in some instances such as:-
- ▶ rejection of an application for a Premises Licence
- ▶ rejection of an application to vary a Premises Licence
- ▶ rejection of an application to transfer a Premises Licence
- ▶ imposition or modification of conditions, excluding a licensable activity, or refusing to specify a person as the Premises Supervisor
- ▶ cancellation of an interim authority notice
- ▶ suspension or revocation of the licence, or removing the Designated Premises Supervisor

A person who made relevant representations or applied for review of the licence and is aggrieved by a licensing authority decision may also appeal. The police having given notice of objection may also appeal against:-

> ▸ a proposed Premises Licence
> ▸ a proposed Designated Premises Supervisor
> ▸ transfer
> ▸ interim authority

An appeal must be made to the magistrates' court for the area in which the premises are situated. Notice of an appeal must be given to the court within 21 days of notification of the relevant decision. A fee is payable.

Club Premises Licence

The provisions for appeal are similar to those for a Premises Licence. Rejection of applications, review and modification of conditions and exclusion of qualifying club activities, variation and withdrawal of a Club Premises Certificate, are all subject to appeal, again within 21 days of notification of the relevant decision.

Temporary Event Notices

The applicant or police aggrieved by a decision may appeal to the magistrates court within 21 days of notification of such a decision. However, no appeal may be brought later than five working days before the day the event period specified in the Temporary Event Notice begins.

Personal Licence

An applicant for a Personal Licence or a Personal Licence holder may appeal against decisions of the licensing authority in cases such as the:-

> ▸ rejection of an application for grant or renewal
> ▸ revocation of a Personal Licence

The police may appeal where they have given notice of objection or convictions have come to light after grant or renewal. The appeal must be made to the magistrates' court for the area in which the licensing authority or any part of it is situated. Notice of appeal must be given to the magistrates within 21 days of notification of the decision.

Where the holder of a Personal Licence gives notice of appeal against a refusal to renew, the magistrates' court hearing the appeal may, on conditions as it may decide, order the licence to continue in force until the appeal is dismissed or abandoned or until it is renewed following a successful appeal.

Closure Orders

Where the magistrates' court has considered a Closure Order instigated by the police, an appeal against any decision made by the court can be made to the Crown Court if notice of it is given to the magistrates within 21 days of their decision.

The holder of a Premises Licence or person who made relevant representations on a review after Closure Order may appeal against a licensing authority Closure Order review decision. The magistrates' court may, on such conditions as it may decide, allow the premises to open pending determination of the appeal.

An appeal must be made to the magistrates' court for the area in which the premises are situated. The appeal notice must be given to the magistrates within 21 days of notification of the decision.

Appealing against a decision

Where an applicant appeals against a decision of the licensing authority, that authority will be the respondent to the appeal. As the appeal will usually be a rehearing of the application, this will mean that the licensing authority may call as witnesses, if they wish to do so, those residents or responsible authorities who gave evidence at the hearing. A resident or responsible authority appealing may for similar reasons need to call as witnesses all those who gave evidence at the hearing.

At the hearing of an appeal the magistrates have three options:-
    a) to dismiss the appeal
    b) to replace the licensing authority's decision by one which the authority could have made
    c) to return the case to the authority with a direction, for example, to re-hear the case in a particular way

It is important to note that the magistrates may decide to go beyond the decision appealed against. They may, for example, extend the period of suspension of a Premises Licence beyond that imposed by the licensing authority at a review hearing. There have already been examples of this where a Premises Licence was suspended after sales were made to under aged persons.

The magistrates may also make an order for costs, which normally would be against a losing party. However a recent directive from the Magistrates' Association and Justices' Clerks Society makes it clear that an award of costs on an appeal should be an exception rather than a rule, and any "resident with reasonable grounds for appeal should not be penalised".

Licensing authorities who act in good faith may be safe from an order for costs against them.

Other Challenges

In addition to the appeal to the magistrates' court on any decision of the licensing authority, there are other possible options to challenge a decision. For example, the decision may be based on the authority's own policy statement, which itself will probably be based on the Guidance. It may be possible to challenge the policy statement, the Guidance, or both, on the basis that they are unlawful. It may be that they contradict the Licensing Act. This could be argued before a magistrates' court on appeal, but it may be more appropriate to put the matter to a higher court.

A challenge of this latter type would be by application to the High Court for a judicial review. Canterbury had the misfortune to be the first licensing authority to have its licensing policy statement put under the microscope of the High Court (see chapter 2).

It would also be possible to challenge any mistake in law made by the magistrates in an appeal hearing. There could, for instance, have been a procedural error or misinterpretation of the rules and regulations. An application could be made to the High Court for a ruling on the matter.

Finally, it is possible that an authority decision may breach human rights and could be challenged on those grounds. For example, everyone is entitled to a fair and public hearing and a right to respect for private and family life and home. An application based on an alleged breach of human rights would be by way of application to the High Court for a judicial review of the offending decision.

12

NOTICES & HEARINGS

Notices

It is important that application notices are served on the right people at the right time. Any failure to comply with the regulations will result in the application being rejected. This will waste both time and money. It may be necessary to start all over again and with some applications this could mean re-advertising and displaying a new application notice.

Notices must comply with the regulations. In some cases there are proper forms, available from the licensing authorities, in hard copy and via their websites, which must be used. Examples are the main application forms for Premises Licenses, Personal Licences, Club Premises Certificates and Temporary Event Notices.

In other cases, such as notices for display and advertisements, regulations specify the size, colour, font size, and contents. Refer to the separate chapters on each type of application for detailed regulations.

Usually the notices and all attachments must be served on everyone on the same day. Addresses can be obtained from the relevant licensing authority and contact details are usually on the authority's website. Applications for a Premises Licence, Provisional Statement, Club Premises Certificate, Variations, and Review require notices to go to the following:-

1) licensing authority
2) police
3) licence holder (review)
4) fire authority
5) health and safety authority
6) planning authority
7) environmental health officer
8) trading standards officer
9) child protection agency

Applications for Transfer, Interim Authority, Variation of Designated Premises Supervisor require notices to go to the following:-
1) licensing authority
2) police
3) Designated Premises Supervisor (variation application)

Applications for a Personal Licence require a notice to go to the licensing authority.

Hearings

A hearing will only take place if an application is met with an objection. Objections are called *relevant representations*. They must be made within a strict time period and can only be made by certain persons and authorities. They must also conform to regulations which state that they must relate to one of the four licensing objectives.

For a detailed explanation reference should be made to chapter 3 and to the chapters dealing with each type of application.

If the objection complies with the requirements, the licensing authority must hold a hearing unless everyone involved agrees that a hearing is unnecessary.

It may be possible for the objections to be satisfied by assurances from the applicant, perhaps by the applicant offering conditions which meet the objection, in which case the objection may subsequently be withdrawn.

So often the first communication between applicant and objector is at the hearing. Many hearings could be avoided if issues are thoroughly discussed when they arise. Where agreement is reached allowing the withdrawal of the objection it is essential that the terms are first recorded in writing between the applicant and objector. Both the applicant and objector should then advise the licensing authority in writing of the terms of the agreement, the objector confirming withdrawal on those terms.

Where a hearing is necessary it must start within a strict period of time.

1. For applications for Premises Licences, Club Premises Certificates, Provisional Statements and variations, there is a period of 28 days for objection starting the day after the local authority receives the applica-

tion. The hearing must start within 20 working days beginning the day after the end of the objection period.

2. For applications for the transfer of Premises Licences, to vary the Designated Premises Supervisor or for Personal Licences, the police have 14 days in which to object starting from the date they received the application notice. The hearing must start within 20 working days beginning the day after the end of the objection period.

3. For applications for interim authority (because of death, incapacity or insolvency), the police have 48 hours from the receipt of the application notice in which to object. The hearing must start within five working days beginning the day after the objection period.

4. For applications for Temporary Event Notices, the police have 48 hours from receipt of the application notice in which to object. The hearing must start within seven working days beginning the day after the objection period ends.

5. For reviews of licences and certificates the police or interested parties have 28 days in which to object, starting the day after the local authority receives the application. The hearing must start within 20 working days beginning the day after the objection period ends.

6. For reviews following Closure Orders, the police or interested parties have seven days in which to object starting the day after the local authority receives the notice of Closure Order from the magistrates' court. The hearing must start within ten working days beginning the day after the end of the period for representations.

7. For a conviction which came to light after the grant or renewal of a Personal Licence, the police have 14 days from receipt of notice from the local authority in which to object. The hearing must start within 20 working days beginning the day after the end of the objection period.

Where hearings last more than one day, they must be heard on consecutive days. They cannot be adjourned part heard, unless the authority considers it necessary for its consideration of any objections or notice made.

The licensing authorities are required to give notice of the hearing to all relevant persons and authorities. In the case of most applications at least ten working days' notice must be given. For a review hearing following a Closure Order the period is five working days.

In the case of Interim Authority applications and Temporary Event Notices at least two working days' notice of the hearing must be given.

The licensing authority does have power to extend the time limits for hearings and other notices if it considers it necessary in the public interest.

The notice of hearing must be accompanied by an explanation of the rights of attendance, assistance, and representation, and rights at the hearing. The licensing authority must also explain the consequence of failure to attend, the procedure at the hearing, and any particular points on which it wants clarification. The notice must be accompanied by a copy of the application notice and copies of relevant representations.

All people and authorities served with the notice of hearing must give to the licensing authority a notice in writing stating whether they intend to attend the hearing and if they consider a hearing unnecessary, to say so. Where they wish to call witnesses they must include a request for permission to call them with a brief explanation of the points on which they may be able to assist.

The notice of attendance must be given in writing at least five working days before the hearing. For Interim Authority and Temporary Event Notice hearings the time is one working day.

Any objections can be withdrawn either at the hearing or by notice in writing given no later than 24 hours before the day of the hearing.

Hearings must be in public, unless the licensing authority considers that, on balance, the public interest is best served by a hearing, or part hearing, in private. Parties may attend the hearing and be represented by any person. For example objectors can be represented by a solicitor or barrister, their ward councillor, and indeed anyone they choose. The only restricted person would be a councillor who was a member of the authority's licensing committee. He should not appear as a representative as clearly there would be a conflict of interest and risk of bias. Parties should give prior notice to the authority of the name of the chosen representative, preferably in their notice of attendance.

A record of the hearing must be taken and kept for six years from the hearing or appeal hearing, whichever is the later.

A member of the licensing authority should not take part in a hearing as a panel member if he/she has a financial interest, either direct or indirect in the application before it, or if his/her involvement would raise a real possibility of bias.

At the hearing the members of the licensing authority can put to those appearing before it, whether applicants, objectors, or other witnesses, any questions they consider relevant. However, those people appearing have no right to question other people, unless the licensing authority agrees.

Those appearing may give further information in response to a prior notice from the licensing authority, and refer to documents produced in support of their position, but documents and information not previously disclosed prior to the hearing may only be referred to with the consent of all parties appearing at the hearing.

The author considers that the information and documentation must be disclosed prior to the day of the hearing - not just minutes before the formal hearing is due to start. The rule is designed to prevent one party surprising another with documents and evidence that the second party has had no time to consider and respond to. Natural justice should prevail and there should be an entitlement to a fair hearing.

With the right to a fair hearing in mind, it is essential that all parties whether the applicant, objectors or responsible authorities such as the police set out in writing, in advance, sufficient details of all the evidence to be relied on. and documents to be disclosed.

In a move in favour of local residents, in the June 2006 review of the Guidance the government made it clear that there is no requirement for an interested party or responsible authority to produce a recorded history of problems at premises to support their representations. There have been numerous horror stories of licensing authorities favouring local residents and police even in cases where no hard evidence of cause for complaint has been provided.

With new applications there can be no such evidence anyway, but there is clear movement from the government's initial position that applications for new premises should be granted and any problems dealt with on review applications.

The licensing authority must disregard irrelevant matters, those which have nothing to do with a party's written case nor with the promotion of the four licensing objectives or, in the case of a police notice, the crime prevention objective.

Where a party fails to attend the hearing having said that they would do so, the authority can either adjourn the hearing, or proceed in the party's absence and consider the written representations.

Can a licensing authority consider issues which relate to one of the licensing objectives but are not raised by any objector - for example an issue which has come to light through evidence at the hearing but not-forming part of the objection? Clearly an authority has no right to intervene except at a hearing but once a hearing is underway the authority is required by the Licensing Act to "carry out its functions ... under this Act ... with a view to promoting the licensing objectives". The strong opinion is that the authority can consider and act on any matter which may undermine one of the licensing objectives.

The authority can decide on its own procedure for the hearing but will start by explaining that procedure to those present and will then consider any written requests made by prior notice for witnesses to be allowed. The hearing will be a discussion led by the authority and each party must be given an equal maximum time to present the case,. This is done by addressing the authority, calling witnesses (if allowed), and questioning another party or their witnesses (if allowed).

One authority at a hearing in which the author himself acted on behalf of the applicant, allowed only ten minutes for 16 objections to be addressed. Subsequently all objectors were given a collective ten minutes to put their case. Whilst this was in accordance with the statutory right of a licensing authority to make provision for rules of evidence at a hearing, such limitation was in the author's opinion against the rules of natural justice and in breach of the parties' rights to a fair hearing under human rights law.

Typically the hearing agenda will provide for an introduction by the licensing officer giving details of the application and objections, a time for each party to present their case followed by questions from other parties, and finally an opportunity for each party to summarise their case. The licensing committee will then retire, together with their legal adviser, but not the licensing officer who should take no part in the decision.

On the committee's return, the legal adviser will usually summarise any advice given to the committee and invite questions on that advice, and finally the committee will give its decision with reasons. Some authorities also provide a written decision with reasons at the hearing. Others send this on to the parties shortly after the hearing.

In every case the authority is required to give details in advance of its procedure, and this should be checked carefully and any concerns raised with the licensing officer.

Where the hearing involves a counter notice following police objection to a Temporary Event Notice or review of a Premises Licence following a Closure Order, the authority must reach a decision at the conclusion of the hearing and give that decision with reasons.

In any other case the authority must make a decision within five working days of the last day of the hearing and must communicate that decision, with reasons, to the parties "forthwith".

The licensing authority has no power to award costs or expenses. Any failure to follow the regulations on hearings or failure to follow its own procedure will not automatically make the hearing void.

13

GAMING, GAMING MACHINES & LOTTERIES

At the time of publication (November 2006) gaming in pubs, clubs, and other venues was governed by the Gaming Act 1968 and lotteries by the Lotteries and Amusements Act 1976. By late 2007 it is expected that the Gambling Act 2005 will be fully in force.

The government aims to have the Act in force by 1st September 2007, but so far there is already a four month delay in publishing the transitional regulations. The detailed regulations dealing with applications forms and fees are due to be published before July 2007.

The Government intends that the new licensing authorities for gambling, effectively the same authorities who now administer the Licensing Act 2003, will be able to accept all applications for licences and permits by early 2007. It was intended that the date by which this would happen would be 31st January but has been put back to 27th April 2007, to allow the new licensing authorities extra time to train and ready themselves for the new applications, sensible in the light of recent experience with the implementation of the Licensing Act. The closing date for transitional applications has also been extended by three months to 31st July 2007.

This chapter will explain the basics of the existing law on gaming machines, gaming generally, and lotteries, and will go on to highlight what can be expected under the new regime. It concentrates on premises licensed for the sale and consumption of alcohol, but does explain the framework for the control of all types of gambling.

The main changes for pubs under the new Act will involve gaming machines, with new authorised categories, numbers, and procedures.

Existing Law

Gaming is prohibited in any public place, subject to specific exceptions which include the following:-

▸ Games of pure skill eg darts, billiards, skittles, and shove ha'penny can be played and gambled on without any restriction on stakes.

▸ Cribbage or dominoes, or any other game specifically authorised by an order of the licensing authority, in any premises which has a Premises Licence under the Licensing Act 2003 authorising the sale of alcohol for consumption on the premises. The relevant licensing authority is the authority which issued the Premises Licence.

▸ Certain gaming other than by machines in members' clubs covered by a licence or registration issued by the gaming committee of the local magistrates' court under Part 11 of the Gaming Act 1968.

▸ Jackpot gaming machines in clubs or miners' welfare institutes authorised by the gaming committee of the local magistrates' court by registration under Part III of the Gaming Act 1968.

▸ Amusement with prizes machines (known as AWP's) where a permit has been issued under Part III of the Gaming Act 1968 by the relevant licensing authority under the Licensing Act 2003, for use of the machines in any premises.

▸ Gaming at entertainment not promoted for private gain, which is not in itself gaming governed by club registration or licensing under the Gaming Act and which is not amusements with prizes under the Lotteries Act (see below), may take place provided the entrance fee or stake per game does not exceed £4, and the total value of all prizes does not exceed £400, and the whole proceeds after deduction of expenses for prizes are applied for purposes other than private gain. Some pubs are using this exemption to host poker tournaments but extreme care must be exercised to ensure legality.

It is an offence for any person under the age of 18 years old to take part in gaming and an offence for the holder of a Premises Licence or anyone employed by him/her or them to knowingly allow a person under the age of 18 to take part in gaming. The maximum fine is £5,000.

It is also an offence for a person under the age of 18 to be in any room of a club where gaming under a Part II licence or registration is taking place.

Lotteries and raffles are generally unlawful, subject to certain exceptions. Unless it comes within the limited exceptions selling raffle tickets in a pub with a prize, for example of a Christmas hamper, cricket bat or any other desirable item, is illegal.

Part II licences and registrations for clubs

For gaming in clubs there are different requirements and procedures for proprietary clubs (owned by someone other than the whole membership collectively) and bona fide members' clubs. Proprietary clubs are licensed, members' clubs are registered, both under Part II of the Gaming Act.

Proprietary clubs require a certificate of consent to apply for a licence issued by the Gaming Board for Great Britain. This will involve a thorough vetting of the proprietors. Genuine members' clubs are relieved of this very high hurdle but must establish that they are a bona fide members' club, have twenty five members or more, are not of a temporary character, and are not principally used for gaming other than bridge or whist or both.

Part III Jackpot machines in clubs etc

Where premises are already licensed or registered for gaming under Part II no further permission is usually required for gaming machines. Where they are not registered or licensed, a genuine members' club or miners' welfare institute can apply for registration under Part III of the Gaming Act 1968 for so-called 'jackpot' machines. Jackpot machines are therefore to be found in casinos, bingo halls and clubs.

The maximum number of jackpot machines per premises is 20, but this is reduced to three where the club or miners' welfare institute is registered under Part II, and to four for bingo club premises.

The maximum stake is £1 per play, (£1 or £2 in casinos, depending on prizes). The maximum payout is £250 for clubs and miners' welfare institutes, £500 for bingo club premises, and £4,000 in casinos.

No machine may be used when the general public have access to the premises.

Application for registration is made in the proper form to the gaming committee of the magistrates' court for the premises. The fee is £115. A copy of the application must be sent to the relevant police officer within seven days. The application will be considered by the next convenient gaming committee meeting, allowing reasonable time for the police to respond. Registration certificates, unless renewed, expire after five years.

A certificate will continue in force until determination of an application for renewal which is made not earlier than six months nor less than six weeks before the certificate is due to expire. The renewal fee is £70. Notice of a renewal application must be given to the relevant police officer within seven days.

The gaming committee has discretion to deal with an application without a hearing where there are no unresolved objections. The committee may refuse to register or renew if it appears that the club is either not a bona fide members' club, has less than twenty five members, or is of a temporary character.

The committee's discretion is absolute and could therefore be exercised against a proprietary club. A number of cases have established that proprietary clubs are likely to be registered if they are under good management, have an established and effective constitution, if the members support the application, and the profits or benefits from the machines are adequately divided between the proprietor and the members.

Amusement with prizes machines (AWPs)

AWP's are machines where there is a maximum stake per play of 50p and where there are any of the following prizes:-

a) a money prize not exceeding £5 (£35 in betting offices, pubs, bingo clubs and amusement arcades)

b) a non-monetary prize not exceeding £8 in value

c) a combination of the money prize and non-monetary prize where the non monetary prize has a maximum value of £8 less the money prize

d) a token prize for playing one or more further games

Conditions b) and c) do not apply where the higher and cash prize only maximum of £35 applies.

There are particular conditions for machines used on amusement machine premises or at a travelling showmen's fair.

AWP machines are licensed by permits but no permit may be issued for club or miners' welfare institutes licensed or registered under Part II of the Gaming Act 1968 (see above). Permits have a maximum duration of three years. They are not transferable. They lapse six months after the death of a holder. Provided application for renewal is made not less than one month before the permit is due to expire, it will continue in force until the application for renewal has been determined by the licensing authority.

Application is made to the local authority for the premises. The fee is £32. The authority may pass a resolution to limit the number of machines on any one premises. A hearing is not necessary unless the authority intends to refuse to grant or renew a permit. The authority has discretion whether to grant (except for amusement machine premises) but must not impose conditions. Under its discretion the authority may refuse on the grounds that because of the use of the premises, the presence of AWP machines should not be allowed, for example because the premises are used mainly by children.

Provided no condition exists where alcohol may only be supplied with food, where an application is made by a Premises Licence holder authorised to supply alcohol for consumption on premises, the machines must be located on the premises where the alcohol is served and consumed. The machines can only be used during the hours that alcohol is supplied.

Lotteries

It is only in very limited circumstances such as with a small lottery, a societies' lottery or amusements with prizes at exempt entertainment, that a lottery can be conducted on premises which have a Premises Licence or Temporary Event Notice under the Licensing Act 2003.

A lottery is a distribution of prizes by lot or chance. Usually it involves some payment for the opportunity to win.

A lottery is unlawful unless it falls within the definition of gaming and is governed by the gaming laws, or is an exemption allowed by the Lotteries and Amusements Act 1976. The exemptions are "small lotteries incidental to exempt entertainment", "private lotteries", "societies' lotteries", "local lotteries", and the National Lottery.

Small lotteries: To qualify under this exemption the lottery must comply with conditions, namely:-

a) no money prizes

b) the tickets must be sold and the result announced during "exempt entertainment" on the premises

c) the lottery is not the only or only substantial, inducement for persons to attend the entertainment

d) other than for payment for printing of tickets, the expense of the entertainment and other authorised expenses including purchases of prizes (maximum £50), the whole of the proceeds of the entertainment and lottery must be given other than for private gain

e) the exempt entertainment must be a bazaar, sale of work, fete, dinner dance, sporting or athletic event or other entertainment of a similar type

Private lotteries: To qualify under this exemption the lottery must be promoted for members of one society established and conducted for purposes not connected with gaming, betting or lotteries, or it must be promoted for people who all work on the same premises.

In addition, the following conditions apply:-

a) the sale of tickets is confined to persons to whom the lottery is promoted and, where it is promoted for a society, any other person on the society's premises

b) the whole of the proceeds after deducting printing costs must be devoted to prizes and/or a society's purposes

c) it may only be published on the premises

d) ticket prices must be the same and printed on the tickets

e) the full price must be received for every ticket

f) the ticket must include the name and address of the promoter and other information

g) tickets must not be sent through the post

Societies' lotteries: To qualify under this exemption, the lottery must be promoted on behalf of a society established and conducted wholly or mainly for one or more of the following:-

a) a charitable purpose

b) athletic sports or games, or cultural activities

c) purposes which are not for private gain or any commercial undertaking

Such a lottery must be promoted in accordance with a scheme approved by the society, and the society must be registered under the Act. The whole proceeds other than expenses such as printing, promotion and prizes, must be applied to the purposes mentioned above. The maximum ticket price is £2, the total value of tickets sold must not exceed £2 million, and no prize may exceed £25,000 or ten per cent of the value of tickets sold.

Local lotteries: These exempt lotteries are those promoted and approved by a local authority and which are registered with the Gaming Board for Great Britain. The same ticket price, sales and prize limits apply as for societies' lotteries.

Amusements with prizes at exempt entertainment: Provided they are not gaming or gaming machines under the Gaming Act 1968, amusements with prizes can be run at "exempt entertainment" namely a bazaar, sale of work, fete, dinner, dance, a sporting or athletic event or any other similar entertainment. The whole proceeds after the expenses of the entertainment must go to purposes other than private gain, and the amusements must not be the only, or only substantial, attraction at the event.

Amusements with prizes at commercial entertainment: In a similar way to amusements at exempt entertainment, amusements with prizes can be provided at certain commercial entertainment where either a permit has been obtained under the Act or where the premises are used mainly for amusement machines under a specific part of the Gaming Act 1968. Again conditions apply.

Gambling Act 2005

The Gambling Act will introduce a very similar structure for gambling to that introduced by the Licensing Act 2003 for sale of alcohol and other activities, with the same key phrases such as Premises Licences, Personal Licences, policy statements, licensing authorities, and a Guidance.

The Act extends to England and Wales and, subject to the exclusion of some provisions, to Scotland. A new unified regulator for betting gaming and lotteries is established, ie the Gambling Commission, which replaces the Gaming Board for Great Britain.

The Commission has a duty to promote the licensing objectives, when carrying out its functions. The Commission is responsible for licensing gambling operators and personnel through operating licences and Personal Licences, and must publish a policy statement setting out the principles, practice, and procedure it will follow in dealing with applications for operating and Personal Licences. The Commission must also publish codes of practice for provision of gambling facilities.

Licensing authorities (local authorities) are responsible for licensing the premises used for gambling, lower stake gaming machines, gaming activities in members' clubs and miners' welfare institutes, authorised gaming in pubs, permits for prize gambling, and registered societies' lotteries.

The Commission is required to publish a Guidance and licensing authorities must have regard to the Guidance in preparing their own policies and in carrying out their functions. Licensing authorities must publish their first policies by 31st January 2007.

All gaming, gaming machines and lotteries will be governed by the new Act. The regulation of AWP machines has already been passed from the magistrates to the licensing authorities under the Licensing Act 2003 with effect 24th November 2005. However, when the Gambling Act 2005 comes into force on 1st September 2007 the licensing authorities will be responsible for all gaming machines and they and the Commission will be responsible for all gambling.

Main changes

The main changes which the Gambling Act 2005 will have on premises involved in the sale and supply of alcohol are:-

- ▶ new licensing authorities take over from the magistrates' courts the responsibility for gaming and gaming machines in clubs and gaming machines in pubs
- ▶ low cost simple procedure to allow up to three gaming machines in premises licensed for and used for sale and consumption of alcohol
- ▶ licensed premises gaming machine permits where more than two machines are required
- ▶ fast track applications for clubs which hold a Club Premises Certificate under the Licensing Act 2003

> provision for transfer of gaming machine permits where more than two machines are required

> extension of gaming allowed in pubs from cribbage and dominoes to all equal chance gaming but subject to conditions including maximum stakes and prize values

Offences

In a similar way to the position under the old legislation, the basic tenet is that gambling is unlawful except in certain highly regulated circumstances. Gambling means gaming, betting, or lotteries as defined by the Act.

The Act creates two distinct offences, with exceptions, and a host of additional offences relating to specific activities. The first of the two main offences concerns the provision of *facilities* for gambling. The second deals with the *use* of premises for specific gambling activities.

The offence of providing facilities does not apply to:-

> an activity covered by an operating licence and carried on in compliance with the terms and conditions of the licence

> provision of facilities for a lottery

> making a gaming machine available for use

> facilities for equal chance gaming by a members' club, commercial club, or a miners' welfare institute, where the relevant conditions are met

> facilities for gaming in accordance with a club gaming permit

> facilities for equal chance gaming on premises (other than a vehicle) which has a Premises Licence for the supply and consumption of alcohol on the premises, contains a bar at which alcohol is served without a condition that it is supplied with food, during the hours authorised for sale, and where relevant conditions are met

> prize gaming either by permit or at entertainment centres. Prize gaming is where neither the nature or size of the prize is determined by the numbers of persons playing or the money raised by the gaming

> private gaming and betting, namely in a private dwelling on a domestic occasion, residential accommodation (eg hostel or student halls of residence) where the public do not have a right of access, and where no charge is made for participation

▶ non-commercial gaming comprising prize gaming or equal chance gaming, at a non-commercial event, where no part of the proceeds after deduction of reasonable event costs or gaming are for private gain, in compliance with conditions

The second and entirely separate offence is the offence of using, without a Premises Licence authorising that activity, premises as a casino, for bingo, for gaming machines, to provide other facilities for gaming, or to provide facilities for betting.

The main exceptions to this offence are:-

▶ an activity covered by a temporary use notice in compliance with the terms and conditions of the notice

▶ making gaming machines available for use on premises which have a Premises Licence for the supply of alcohol for consumption on the premises, provided that either no more than two machines in categories C and D (see later) are made available and notice is given to the licensing authority, or machines in those categories are provided in accordance with a licensed premises gaming machine permit

▶ gaming machines which do not provide an opportunity to win a prize or the prize value does not exceed the amount paid to use the machine

▶ equal chance gaming by clubs and miners' welfare institutes, subject to conditions

▶ gaming in accordance with a club gaming permit

▶ gaming machines under a club gaming machine permit

▶ equal chance gaming on premises with an alcohol licence (see above)

▶ Category D gaming machines under a family entertainment centre gaming machine permit (see later)

▶ Travellers' fairs

▶ Prize gaming

▶ Private gaming and betting

▶ Non-commercial gaming

The penalties on conviction are a prison sentence of up to 51 weeks, a fine up to £5,000, or both.

Gaming

Operating licences

Operating licences are issued by the Gambling Commission to an individual or body (the term 'a person' covers both) and where that person is an individual he/she must be aged 18 or over and can authorise:-
1. a casino (a casino operating licence)
2. bingo (bingo operating licence)
3. betting (general betting operating licence)
4. pool betting (pool betting operating licence)
5. gaming machines in adult gaming centre (gaming machine general operating licence)
6. gaming machines in family entertainment centres (gaming machine general operating licence)
7. promotion of a lottery (lottery operating licence)
8. manufacture supply installation and maintenance/repair of gaming machines (gaming machine technical operating licence)
9. manufacture supply installation and adaption of gambling software (gambling software operating licence maintenance)

Application is made to the Commission, and specific information will be required in a prescribed form, with the relevant fee. At the time of publication the regulations dealing with forms, fees and service of documents are yet to be made but the main regulations are expected to be published by the end of 2006 to enable applications to be made from early 2007, with the balance of the regulations coming by July 2007. In considering the application the Commission must have regard to:
▶ the licensing objectives
▶ the applicant's suitability to carry on the licensed activities
▶ the suitability of any gaming machines

The licensing objectives are:-
a) preventing gambling from being a source of crime and disorder, being associated with crime or disorder or being used to support crime
b) ensuring that gambling is conducted in a fair and open way
c) protecting children and other vulnerable persons from being harmed or exploited by gambling. Curiously, unlike the Licensing Act 2003, there is no mention of public nuisance or public safety.
The Commission must maintain a statement identifying the kind of

evidence they will look to and take into account in assessing integrity, competency, and financial integrity of an applicant, and suitability of gaming machines.

The Commission may refuse an application if the applicant has a conviction for a relevant offence and may take into account the expected demand for the facilities. The licence may limit the number of sets of premises on which the licensed activities may be carried on, and may limit the number of persons for whom facilities may be provided on any premises where the licensed activities are carried on.

The Commission may grant or reject the application, grant only one or more of the activities requested, or grant subject to conditions. It must as soon as possible advise the applicant of its decision.

Generally an operating licence will continue in force indefinitely, but the Commission may impose a condition limiting the duration of the licence. An annual fee is payable and the licence may be the subject of variation, renewal, surrender, forfeiture (by a court on conviction of a relevant offence), review, suspension or revocation after review. It will lapse if the licensee dies, becomes mentally or physically incapable of carrying on the licensed activities, or becomes insolvent.

Appeals must be made to the Gambling Appeals Tribunal and must be lodged within one month of the decision appealed against, although the Tribunal does have power to accept a late appeal. Further appeal may be made to the High Court on a point of law.

Premises Licences

Where the exceptions do not apply, any gambling involving the use of any premises for a casino, bingo, gaming machines, facilities for gaming or betting, must be in accordance with an operating licence and a Premises Licence.

A Premises Licence may authorise:-

- ▶ the operation of a casino ("casino operating licence")
- ▶ facilities for bingo ("bingo premises licence")
- ▶ Category B gaming machines ("adult gaming centre premises licence")
- ▶ Category C gaming machines ("family entertainment centre premises licence")

▸ facilities for betting ("betting premises licence")

Application is made to the licensing authority, which is the same as the authority established under the Licensing Act 2003 to deal with licensing of sale of alcohol, regulated entertainment, and late night refreshment.

The licensing authority must not consider demand when exercising their functions, and need only consider codes of practice and Guidance from the Gambling Commission, the licensing objectives, and their own policy statement, "as the authority think fit". This would appear to give them an extraordinary amount of discretion, a position very different from that under the Licensing Act 2003.

The applicant must have a right to occupy the premises and must hold or have applied for an operating licence. Regulations will be made dealing with service and publication of the application. Interested parties and responsible authorities may make objections in much the same way as provided for under the Licensing Act 2003. Where objections cannot be resolved a hearing must take place. Conditions may be applied either by regulation or the licensing authority after a hearing.

There are limits to the number of gaming machines which may be authorised, depending on the type of premises and category of gaming machine.

Provision is made for the transfer and variation of a Premises Licence, payment of annual fees, and production of the licence. Regulations may also limit the duration of a Premises Licence.

A licence may be surrendered or revoked for non-payment of fees. It will lapse if the holder dies, suffers mental or physical incapacity, or becomes insolvent.

A Premises Licence may be reviewed on application by a responsible authority or interested party or, following notice of review, by the licensing authority.

Again, in much the same way as under the Licensing Act 2003, there is a mechanism for applying for a provisional statement for premises yet to be constructed, where alterations are proposed, or a right to occupy expected.

Appeals are to the magistrates' court within 21 days of notification of the decision appealed against.

Personal Licences

The Gambling Commission may attach a condition to an operating licence requiring a least one person occupying a specified management office, for example a director of a company or partner in a business, to hold a Personal Licence. A Personal Licence will authorise the individual to carry out those functions in connection with the provision of facilities for gambling or a person who provides those facilities.

'Small-scale operators', yet to be defined, are exempt from a requirement for someone to hold a Personal Licence.

Application is made to the Gambling Commission.

A Personal Licence has an unlimited duration, but may be suspended by the Gambling Commission, surrendered, forfeited by a court on conviction of a relevant offence or revoked by the Gambling Commission. It will lapse in the event of death, insolvency, or mental or physical incapacity. There are requirements for production to a police constable or enforcement officer.

Appeals must be made to the Gambling Appeals Tribunal, and must be lodged within one month of the decision appealed against, although the Tribunal does have power to accept a late appeal. Further appeal on a point of law may be made to the High Court .

Temporary use notices

A temporary use notice will allow the holder of an operating licence to carry on activities authorised by that licence on premises which are not covered by the licence.

Premises may not be used under a temporary use notice for more than 21 days in a twelve month period. The notice in the prescribed form must be given to the licensing authority more than three months before it is due to apply, must be accompanied by a copy of the notice and the fee, and copies must be served within seven days on the Gambling Commission, police, and HM Revenue & Customs. The licensing authority must acknowledge receipt.

If no notice of objection is received within 14 days of receipt of the notice, the licensing authority must endorse the notice and return it to the applicant.

If notice of objection is given by the licensing authority itself, the

Gambling Commission, police, or HM Revenue & Customs, within the 14 day period, then the whole procedure explained below must be completed within a six week period from the date when the licensing authority received the temporary use notice.

Any notice of objection must be given to the applicant and copied to the licensing authority. If the objection is not withdrawn, and there is no agreement to a modification, a hearing must be held. If the licensing authority, after the hearing, thinks that the temporary use notice should not be allowed to take effect, or should have effect only with modifications, they may give a counter-notice to the applicant.

An appeal, either by the person who gave the notice or those entitled to receive it, must be made to the magistrates' court within 14 days of receipt of the relevant notification.

Once issued the notice must be displayed on the relevant premises when the authorised activities are taking place, and must be produced to authorised officers on request.

Gaming machines

Under the Act there are four categories of gaming machine, A, B, C and D. Category B is further sub-divided. The regulations will identify for each category:-

▶ the cost of playing the machine
▶ the value of prizes
▶ the type of prize
▶ the type of gambling
▶ the premises where they may be used

Category A machines will have an unlimited stake, an unlimited maximum prize, and the maximum of all categories of machines is not more than 25 times the number of gaming tables and 1250 per premises. Category A machines are only allowed in regional casinos.

Category B machines are likely to be divided into four categories.

It is proposed that B1 machines will have a maximum £1 stake, with a maximum prize of £2,000; B2 machines will probably have a maximum stake of £100 per game or £15 per chip, and have a maximum prize of £500; B3 machines will probably have a maximum stake of £1 and a maximum prize of £500; B4 machines will probably have a maximum stake of £1 and a maximum prize of £250.

Category C machines will probably have a maximum stake of £1 and a maximum prize of £35.

Category D machines will probably have a maximum stake of 10p (30p where non-exchangeable prizes) and a maximum prize of £5 (cash or non cash).

The numbers of machines of each category allowed per premises will be dependent on the type of premises. For example Category A machines are only allowed in regional casinos, and then in limited numbers. The restrictions are as follows:-

▶ Adult gaming centres: up to four Category B machines and any number of Category C and D machines

▶ Licensed family entertainment centres: Category C and D machines of any number

▶ Casinos: small casinos may have a maximum of two machines of Category B, C or D per gaming table subject to a maximum of 80 in all. Large casinos may have up to five of these machines per table with an overall maximum of 150. Regional casinos with at least 40 tables may have 25 machines of any category per gaming table with an overall maximum of 1250

▶ Bingo premises: up to four Category B machines, and any number of Category C and D machines

▶ Betting premises: up to four machines of category B, C or D

▶ Tracks: where pool betting is permitted, up to four machines of Category B, C or D

▶ Clubs and pubs: see later in this chapter

An offence is committed by a person who makes a gaming machine available for use by another, unless it is under an operating licence or covered by one of the exceptions explained below.

There are offences relating to the manufacture, supply, installation, adaption, maintenance or repair, except under an operating licence or in certain circumstances. The exceptions are:-

▶ Category D gaming machines under a family entertainment centre gaming machine permit

▶ Gaming machines which do not give an opportunity to win a prize

▶ Gaming machines which do not give an opportunity to win a prize greater in value to the amount paid to play the machine

▶ Gaming machines covered by a club gaming permit

▶ Gaming machines covered by a club machine permit

▶ Gaming machines of a certain type and number on premises licensed to sell alcohol for consumption on the premises

▶ Gaming machines covered by a licensed premises gaming machine permit

▶ Gaming machines at travelling fairs

Clubs

It is not unlawful to provide equal chance gaming in members' clubs, commercial clubs (also known as proprietary clubs), and miners' welfare institutes, as defined by the Act, provided certain conditions are met including maximum stakes and prizes and membership provisions.

Other gaming may be authorised by a club gaming permit issued by the licensing authority allowing provision of facilities for gaming on members' club or miners' welfare institute premises as part of their activities. Note that this does not apply to commercial clubs, which will have to proceed by applying for an operating licence. A club gaming permit will allow:-

▶ up to three gaming machines in Categories B,C or D

▶ facilities for equal chance gaming subject to conditions (but no maximum stake or prize value)

▶ facilities for games of chance subject to regulations and conditions, including conditions that the public, children and young persons are excluded from the area where gaming is taking place

A club gaming permit is subject to conditions that a member must have applied for or have been nominated for membership or become member at least 48 hours before taking part in the gaming, or be a guest of such a person.

Further conditions provide that no child or young person will use a Category B or C gaming machine and that the holder will comply with any code of practice issued by the Gambling Commission dealing with the location and operation of machines.

Commercial clubs, and members' clubs and miners' welfare institutes who do not have a club gaming permit, may apply for a club gaming machine permit to allow up to three gaming machines of either category B,C or D. Similar conditions to club gaming permits apply regarding membership and children.

The procedure for applying for club gaming permits and club gaming machine permits is the same. Application is made to the licensing authority on the prescribed form, with required documents and fees, and copies must be sent to the Gambling Commission and the police. The Gambling Commission and police may object. The licensing authority may reject the application for a number of reasons, but must first hold a hearing. They may not attach conditions to a permit.

There is a fast track procedure for holders of Club Premises Certificates under the Licensing Act 2003. They do not have to serve the Gambling Commission or police, who may not object. There are limited grounds for rejection, for example where the club's main activity is gaming.

There is an obligation to keep the permit on the premises and to produce it to the police or enforcement officer on demand. The permit will last ten years, and an annual fee is payable. A permit may be surrendered and renewed (apply not more than three months but not later than six weeks before expiry), and in certain circumstances may be cancelled by the licensing authority, for example if an offence has been committed or the premises are used wholly or mainly by children or young persons.

A permit will lapse if the club ceases to be a members' club (even if it becomes a commercial club), commercial club or miners' welfare institute.

Appeals are made to the magistrates' court within 21 days of receiving the notice of relevant decision.

Pubs and other premises licensed and used for consumption of alcohol

There are special arrangements for premises which have the benefit of a Premises Licence under the Licensing Act 2003 authorising the sale of alcohol for consumption on the premises, which have a bar at which alcohol is served without a condition that is served with food and which apply during the hours authorised for supply of alcohol.

Firstly, equal chance gaming may take place on the premises subject to conditions including the amount of stake and value of the prize and exclusion of children and young persons from the gaming. Examples are cribbage and dominoes.

Secondly, up to two machines of either Category C or D may be provided for use on the premises. However, the holder of the Premises Licence must give written notice to the licensing authority, pay the prescribed fee, and comply with any code issued by the Gambling Commission dealing with the location and operation of machines.

These two special arrangements may be removed by a licensing authority if they think they are not consistent with the licensing objectives, gaming has taken place in breach of conditions, the premises are mainly used for gaming, or an offence under the Gambling Act has been committed on the premises. However, the authority must give 21 days' notice consider representations and hold a hearing if requested. Appeal may be made to the magistrates' court within 21 days of receipt of the order appealed against.

Thirdly, these premises may apply for a licensed premise gaming machine permit authorising Category C or D machines of any number. Application is made by the Premises Licence holder to the licensing authority in the prescribed form with the relevant fee. The authority must not attach conditions to the permit, but must grant it (subject only to the number and type of machines, in which case they must invite representations) or refuse it having regard to the licensing objectives, the Guidance issued by the Gambling Commission, and other matters they feel are relevant.

There is a requirement to keep a permit on the premises, to produce it to a police officer or enforcement/local authority officer, and to pay an annual fee. The permit will continue in force until the premises cease to have an on-premises alcohol licence or the holder of the permit ceases to be the holder of the licence. It may be varied on application.

The licensing authority has power to cancel or vary the permit, for example where offences have been committed, but must give the holder 21 days' notice, consider representations, and hold a hearing if one is requested. A decision will not take effect until the appeal period of 21 days has expired or the appeal (to the magistrates' court) disposed of. A court may forfeit the permit where the holder is convicted of a relevant offence.

Any person applying for the transfer of a Premises Licence authorising the supply of alcohol for consumption on the premises, may also apply for the transfer to him of any licensed premises gaming machine permit. There is provision for the application for the transfer to have interim effect where application has been made for the transfer of the Premises Licence to have interim effect.

Lotteries

Except where a person has an operating licence authorising the lottery, or acts on behalf of someone who has, or the lottery is an exempt lottery, it is illegal to promote a lottery, in other words to participate in any of the arrangements for a lottery, or to facilitate a lottery.

A lottery is an exempt lottery if it is part of a non-commercial event, a private lottery, a customer lottery, or a small society lottery.

Non-commercial lotteries: the lottery must not in any way be promoted for private gain. No sum raised, after deduction only of a prescribed sum for the cost of prizes and prescribed expenses, may be used for private gain. No rollover is allowed. Tickets may only be sold at the event whilst it is taking place, and the result must be announced at the event.

Private lotteries: a private society lottery, a work lottery, or a residents' lottery. No rollovers or profits are allowed, they may only be advertised on the relevant premises, and tickets must be paid for up front and show the name and address of the promoter and ticket price which must be the same for each ticket.

A private society lottery as the name implies is one promoted for and by members of a society, although anyone on the society's premises may take part. The society must not be connected to gambling.

A work lottery is one promoted for and by people working on the same premises (or contracted to work at those and perhaps other premises).

A residents' lottery is one promoted for and by people who live at the same premises. For example, student halls of residence.

Customer lotteries: This is a lottery run by a business for customers on their premises. There is a maximum prize of £50, no profit may be made, and the lottery can only be advertised on the premises. No rollover is allowed, and the tickets must be paid for up front and show the name and address of the promoter and ticket price which must be the same for each ticket. Draws must not take place more frequently than every seven days. **Small society lotteries:** The society must be registered with the licensing authority. There will be an annual fee. The society must not be commercial, the proceeds of a single lottery must not exceed £20,000 and all lotteries £250,000 in any one calendar year, at least 20 per cent of the proceeds must go to the purpose for which the society is conducted, and the maximum prize is £25,000.

There are conditions on tickets and filing records as well as provisions for revocation, cancellation, and appeal.

Where exemptions do not apply, anyone wishing to promote a lottery must obtain an operating licence from the Gambling Commission authorising the lottery (see above).

Prize gaming

A permit can be obtained to authorise prize gaming, where it is not already covered by any other authority for gaming under the Act.

Prize gaming is defined as gaming where neither the type nor size of prize is decided by the number of players or the amount of takings. In other words the prize is put up in advance, an example being types of bingo played in amusement arcades.

Prize gaming is also permitted in adult gaming centres, licensed family entertainment centres, bingo halls, and at travelling fairs.

When a permit is required, application is made to the licensing authority, by a company, organisation or person aged 18 or over. A permit lasts for ten years, but will lapse if the holder ceases to occupy the premises, if an individual dies becomes bankrupt or physically or mentally incapable, and if an organisation or company ceases to exist or becomes insolvent.

There is provision for surrender of the permit, forfeiture by a court, and renewal.

Private and non-commercial gaming and betting

Provision of facilities or using premises for private gaming and betting is not illegal. Private gaming is equal chance gaming which takes place where the public do not have access, and other gaming which is domestic or residential.

Domestic means in a private dwelling on a domestic occasion. Residential means in a hall or hostel where more than half of the players are residents. No charge may be made and the public must not have access.

Private betting is where the betting takes place on premises where each party to the betting transaction lives, or at work between people employed by the same employer.

Gaming at an event where no part of the proceeds is to be used for private gain is lawful in certain circumstances and subject to certain conditions. For example, non-commercial prize gaming is lawful where the players are advised of the aim to raise money for a specific purpose, for example a charitable cause, where profits after deduction of reasonable expenses are given to that cause, provided also that the premises are not at the same time subject to a Premises Licence or temporary use notice.

Non-commercial equal chance gaming has additional conditions limiting by regulation the amount of stakes and value of prizes.

Transitional provisions

Regulations will be made dealing with conversion of existing licences and authorisations, and in some cases continuation of old licences and authorisations until they expire or new licences granted, and also or applying for new licences and authorisations before the new Act comes into force on 1st September 2007.

Advance applications for Premises Licenses may be made from 27th April 2007, and existing operators who apply by 31st July 2007 will be able to continue operating after 31st August 2007 even if the Licensing Authority have not by that date dealt with their application.

Annex D

Conditions relating to the prevention of crime and disorder

It should be noted in particular that it is unlawful under the 2003 Act:

- knowingly to sell or supply or attempt to sell or supply alcohol to a person who is drunk
- knowingly to allow disorderly conduct on licensed premises
- for the holder of a premises licence or a designated premises supervisor knowingly to keep or to allow to be kept on licensed premises any goods that have been imported without payment of duty or which have otherwise been unlawfully imported
- to allow the presence of children under 16 who are not accompanied by an adult between midnight and 5am at any premises licensed for the sale of alcohol for consumption on the premises, and at any time in premises used exclusively or primarily for the sale and consumption of alcohol

Conditions enforcing these arrangements are therefore unnecessary.

General

When applicants for premises licences or club premises certificates are preparing their operating schedules or club operating schedules, when responsible authorities are considering such applications and when licensing authorities are considering applications following the receipt of any relevant representations from a responsible authority or interested party, the following options should be considered as measures which, if necessary, would promote the prevention of crime and disorder.

Whether or not any risk assessment shows these options to be necessary in the individual circumstances of any premises will depend on a range of factors including the nature and style of the venue, the activities being conducted there, the location of the premises and the anticipated clientele of the business involved. It should also be borne in mind that club premises operate under codes of discipline to ensure the good order and behaviour of members.

Necessary conditions for the licence or certificate will also depend on local knowledge of the premises.

Under no circumstances should the following measures be regarded as standard conditions to be automatically imposed in all cases. They are designed to provide a range of possible conditions drawn from experience relating to differing situations and to offer guidance.

Any individual preparing an operating schedule is at liberty to volunteer any measure, such as those described below, as a step he or she intends to take to promote the licensing objectives. When incorporated into the licence or certificate as a condition, they become enforceable under the law and a breach of such a condition could give rise to prosecution.

The Licensing Handbook

Text/Radio pagers

Text and radio pagers connecting premises licence holders, designated premises supervisors, managers of premises and clubs to the local police can provide for rapid response by the police to situations of disorder which may be endangering the customers and staff on the premises.

Such pagers provide two-way communication, both enabling licence holders, managers, designated premises supervisors and clubs to report incidents to the police, and enabling the police to warn those operating a large number of other premises of potential trouble-makers or individuals suspected of criminal behaviour who are about in a particular area. Pager systems can also be used by licence holders, door supervisors, managers, designated premises supervisors and clubs to warn each other of the presence in an area of such people.

The Secretary of State recommends that text or radio pagers should be considered appropriate necessary conditions for public houses, bars and nightclubs operating in city and town centre leisure areas with a high density of licensed premises. Following individual consideration of the particular circumstances of the venue, such conditions may also be appropriate and necessary in other areas for the prevention of crime and disorder.

It is recommended that a condition requiring the text/radio pager links to the police should include the following elements:

- a requirement that the text/pager equipment is kept in working order at all times;
- a requirement that the pager link be activated, made available to and monitored by the designated premises supervisor or a responsible member of staff at all times that the premises are open to the public;
- a requirement that any police instructions/directions are complied with whenever given; and
- a requirement that all instances of crime or disorder are reported via the text/radio pager link by the designated premises supervisor or a responsible member of staff to an agreed police contact point.

Door supervisors

Conditions relating to the provision of door supervisors and security teams may be valuable in:

- preventing the admission and ensuring the departure from the premises of the drunk and disorderly, without causing further disorder;
- keeping out excluded individuals (subject to court bans or imposed by the licence holder);
- searching and excluding those suspected of carrying illegal drugs, or carrying offensive weapons; and
- maintaining orderly queuing outside of venues prone to such queuing.

Where door supervisors conducting security activities are to be a condition of a licence, which means that they would have to be registered with the Security Industry Authority, conditions may also need to deal with the number of such supervisors, the displaying of name badges, the carrying of proof of registration, where and at what times they should be stationed on the premises, and whether at least one female supervisor should be available (for example, if female customers are to be the subject of body searches). Door supervisors also have a role to play in ensuring public safety (see Annex E).

Bottle bans

Glass bottles may be used as weapons inflicting more serious harm during incidents of disorder. A condition can prevent sales of drinks in glass bottles for consumption on the premises.

It is recommended that a condition requiring that no sales of beverages in glass bottles for consumption on the premises should be expressed in clear terms and include the following elements:

- no bottles containing beverages of any kind, whether open or sealed, shall be given to customers on the premises whether at the bar or by staff service away from the bar;
- no customers carrying open or sealed bottles shall be admitted to the premises at any time that the premises are open to the public (**note:** this needs to be carefully worded where off-sales also take place);

In appropriate circumstances, the condition could include exceptions, for example, as follows:

- but bottles containing wine may be sold for consumption with a table meal by customers who are seated in an area set aside from the main bar area for the consumption of food.

Plastic containers and toughened glass

Glasses containing drinks may be used as weapons during incidents of disorder and in untoughened form, can cause very serious injuries. Consideration could therefore be given to conditions requiring either the use of plastic containers or toughened glass which inflicts less severe injuries where considered necessary. Location and style of the venue and the activities carried on there would be particularly important in assessing whether a condition is necessary. For example, the use of glass containers on the terraces of some outdoor sports grounds may obviously be of concern, and similar concerns may also apply to indoor sports events such as boxing matches. Similarly, the use of such plastic containers or toughened glass during the televising of live sporting events, such as international football matches, when high states of excitement and emotion fuelled by alcohol might arise, may be a necessary condition.

It should be noted that the use of plastic or paper drinks containers and toughened glass may also be relevant as measures necessary to promote public safety (see Annex E).

CCTV

The presence of CCTV cameras can be an important means of deterring and detecting crime at and immediately outside licensed premises. Conditions should not just consider a requirement to have CCTV on the premises, but also the precise siting of each camera, the requirement to maintain cameras in working order, and to retain recordings for an appropriate period of time.

The police should provide individuals conducting risk assessments when preparing operating schedules with advice on the use of CCTV to prevent crime.

Open containers not to be taken from the premises

Drinks purchased in licensed premises or clubs may be taken from those premises for consumption elsewhere. Where premises are licensed for the sale of alcohol for consumption off the premises that would be entirely lawful. However, consideration should be given to a condition preventing the taking of alcoholic and other drinks from the premises in open containers (e.g. glasses and opened bottles). This may again be necessary to prevent the use of these containers as offensive weapons in surrounding streets after individuals have left the premises.

Restrictions on drinking areas

It may be necessary to restrict the areas where alcoholic drinks may be consumed in premises after they have been purchased from the bar. An example would be at a sports ground where the police consider it necessary to prevent the consumption of alcohol on the terracing of sports grounds during particular sports events. Such conditions should not only specify these areas, but indicate the circumstances in which the ban would apply and times at which it should be enforced.

Capacity limits

Although most commonly made a condition of a licence on public safety grounds, consideration should also be given to conditions which set capacity limits for licensed premises or clubs where it may be necessary to prevent overcrowding which can lead to disorder and violence. Where such a condition is considered necessary, consideration should also be given to whether door supervisors would be needed to ensure that the numbers are appropriately controlled.

Proof of age cards

It is unlawful for children under 18 to attempt to buy alcohol just as it is unlawful to sell or supply alcohol to them. To prevent such crimes, it may be necessary to require a policy to be applied at certain licensed premises requiring the production of "proof of age" before such sales are made. This should not be limited to recognised "proof of age" cards, but allow for the production of other proof, such as photo-driving licences, student cards and passports. The Secretary of State strongly supports the PASS accreditation system (see paragraph 12.8 of the Guidance) which aims to approve and accredit various proof of age schemes that are in existence. This ensures that such schemes maintain high standards, particularly in the area of integrity and security, and where appropriate and necessary, conditions may refer directly to PASS accredited proof of age cards, photo-driving licences and passports.

It should be noted that many adults in England and Wales do not currently carry any proof of age. This means that the wording of any condition will require careful thought. For example, the requirement might be to ensure sight of evidence of age from any person appearing to those selling or supplying alcohol to be under the age of 18 and who is attempting to buy alcohol. This would ensure that most minors – even those looking older – would need to produce proof of age appropriately before making such a purchase. Under such an arrangement only a minority of adults might be affected, but for the majority there would be no disruption to their normal activity, for example, when shopping in a supermarket.

Crime prevention notices

It may be necessary at some premises for notices to be displayed which warn customers of the prevalence of crime which may target them. Some premises may be reluctant to volunteer the display of such notices for commercial reasons. For example, in certain areas, a condition attached to a premises licence or club premises certificate might require the displaying of notices at the premises which warn customers about the need to be aware of pickpockets or bag snatchers, and to guard their property. Similarly, it may be necessary for notices to be displayed which advise customers not to leave bags unattended because of concerns about terrorism. Consideration could be given to a condition requiring a notice to display the name of a contact for customers if they wish to report concerns.

Drinks promotions

Standardised conditions should not be attached to premises licences or club premises certificates which promote fixed prices for alcoholic drinks. It is also likely to be unlawful for licensing authorities or police officers to promote voluntary arrangements of this kind. This can risk creating cartels. Using conditions to control the prices of alcoholic drinks in an area may also breach competition law. Conditions tailored to the individual circumstances of particular premises which address **irresponsible** drinks promotions may be permissible provided they are necessary for the promotion of the licensing objectives, but licensing authorities should take their own legal advice before a licence or certificate is granted in that form. Judgements may be subjective, and on occasions, there will be a very fine line between responsible and irresponsible promotions but an even greater distinction to whether the promotion in question can be subject to the imposition of a condition. It is therefore vital that such matters are considered objectively in the context of the licensing objectives and with the benefit of appropriate legal advice.

In addition, when considering any relevant representations which demonstrate a clear causal link between sales promotions or discounting and levels of crime and disorder on or in the vicinity of the premises, it would be appropriate for the licensing authority to consider whether the imposition of a new condition prohibiting irresponsible sales promotions or discounting of prices of alcoholic beverages is necessary at those premises. However, before pursuing any form of restrictions at all, licensing authorities should take their own legal advice.

Signage

It may be necessary for the normal hours under the terms of the premises licence or club premises certificate at which licensable activities are permitted to take place to be displayed on or immediately outside the premises so that it is clear if breaches of the terms of the licence or certificate are taking place.

Similarly, it may be necessary for any restrictions on the admission of children to be displayed on or immediately outside the premises so that the consequences of breaches of these conditions would also be clear and to deter those who might seek admission in breach of those conditions.

Large capacity venues used exclusively or primarily for the "vertical" consumption of alcohol (HVVDs)

Large capacity "vertical drinking" premises, sometimes called High Volume Vertical Drinking establishments (HVVDs), are premises with exceptionally high capacities, used primarily or exclusively for the sale and consumption of alcohol, and have little or no seating for patrons.

Where necessary and appropriate, conditions can be attached to premises licences for the promotion of the prevention of crime and disorder at such premises (if not volunteered by the venue operator and following representations on such grounds) which require adherence to:

- a prescribed capacity;
- an appropriate ratio of tables and chairs to customers based on the capacity; and
- the presence of SIA registered security teams to control entry for the purpose of compliance with the capacity limit.

The Licensing Handbook

Annex E

Conditions relating to public safety (including fire safety)

It should be noted that conditions relating to public safety should be those which are necessary, in the particular circumstances of any individual premises or club premises, and should not duplicate other requirements of the law. Equally, the attachment of conditions to a premises licence or club premises certificate will not in any way relieve employers of the statutory duty to comply with the requirements of other legislation including the Health and Safety at Work etc. Act 1974, associated regulations and especially the requirements under the Management of Health and Safety at Work Regulations 1999 and the Fire Precautions (Workplace) Regulations 1997 to undertake risk assessments. Employers should assess the risks, including risks from fire, and take measures necessary to avoid and control these risks. Conditions enforcing those requirements would therefore be unnecessary.

General

When applicants for premises licences or club premises certificates are preparing their operating schedules or club operating schedules, responsible authorities are considering such applications and licensing authorities are considering applications following the receipt of relevant representations from a responsible authority or interested party, the following options should be considered as measures that, if necessary, would promote public safety. Additional matters relating to cinemas and theatres are considered in Annex F. It should also be recognised that special issues may arise in connection with outdoor and large scale events.

Whether or not any risk assessment shows any of the measures to be necessary in the individual circumstances of any premises will depend on a range of factors including the nature and style of the venue, the activities being conducted there, the location of the premises and the anticipated clientele of the business involved.

Necessary conditions for the licence or certificate will also depend on local knowledge of the premises.

In addition, to considering the points made in this Annex, those preparing operating schedules or club operating schedules, licensing authorities and responsible authorities should consider:

*   Model National and Standard Conditions for Places of Public Entertainment and Associated Guidance ISBN 1 904031 11 0 (Entertainment Technology Press – ABTT Publications)
*   The Event Safety Guide – A guide to health, safety and welfare at music and similar events (HSE 1999)("The Purple Book") ISBN 0 7176 2453 6
*   Managing Crowds Safely (HSE 2000) ISBN 0 7176 1834 X
*   5 Steps to Risk Assessment: Case Studies (HSE 1998) ISBN 07176 15804
*   The Guide to Safety at Sports Grounds (The Stationery Office, 1997) ("The Green Guide") ISBN 0 11 300095 2

*   Safety Guidance for Street Arts, Carnival, Processions and Large Scale Performances published by the Independent Street Arts Network, copies of which may be obtained through: **www.streetartsnetwork.org.uk/pages/publications.htm**
*   The London District Surveyors Association's "Technical Standards for Places of Public Entertainment" ISBN 0 9531229 2 1

The following British Standards should also be considered:

*   BS 5588 Part 6 (regarding places of assembly)
*   BS 5588 Part 9 (regarding ventilation and air conditioning systems)
*   BS 5588 Part 9 (regarding means of escape for disabled people)
*   BS 5839 (fire detection, fire alarm systems and buildings)
*   BS 5266 (emergency lighting systems)

110

However, in consulting these texts, which were prepared prior to the coming into force of the Licensing Act 2003, those creating operating schedules or club operating schedules, licensing authorities and responsible authorities should again note that under no circumstances should any conditions be regarded as standard for all premises.

Any individual preparing an operating schedule or club operating schedule is at liberty to volunteer any measure, such as those described below, as a step he or she intends to take to promote the licensing objectives. When incorporated into the licence or certificate as a condition, they become enforceable under the law and a breach of such a condition could give rise to prosecution.

Disabled people

In certain premises where existing legislation does not provide adequately for the safety of the public, consideration might also be given to conditions that ensure that:

- when disabled people are present, adequate arrangements exist to enable their safe evacuation in the event of an emergency; and
- disabled people on the premises are made aware of those arrangements.

Escape routes

It may be necessary to include conditions relating to the maintenance of all escape routes and exits including external exits. These might be expressed in terms of the need to ensure that such exits are kept unobstructed, in good order with non-slippery and even surfaces, free of trip hazards and clearly identified. In restaurants and other premises where chairs and tables are provided this might also include ensuring that internal gangways are kept unobstructed.

In certain premises where existing legislation does not provide adequately for the safety of the public, consideration might also be given to conditions that ensure that:

- all exits doors are easily openable without the use of a key, card, code or similar means;
- doors at such exits are regularly checked to ensure that they function satisfactorily and a record of the check kept;
- any removable security fastenings are removed whenever the premises are open to the public or occupied by staff;
- all fire doors are maintained effectively self-closing and shall not be held open other than by approved devices (for example, electromagnetic releases operated by smoke detectors);
- fire resisting doors to ducts, service shafts, and cupboards shall be kept locked shut; and
- the edges of the treads of steps and stairways are maintained so as to be conspicuous.

Safety checks

In certain premises where existing legislation does not provide adequately for the safety of the public or club members and guests, consideration might also be given to conditions that ensure that:

- safety checks are carried out before the admission of the public; and
- details of such checks are kept in a Log-book.

Curtains, hangings, decorations and upholstery

In certain premises where existing legislation does not provide adequately for the safety of the public or club members and guests, consideration might also be given to conditions that ensure that:

- hangings, curtains and temporary decorations are maintained in a flame-retardant condition;
- any upholstered seating meets on a continuous basis the pass criteria for smouldering ignition source 0, flaming ignition source 1 and crib ignition source 5 when tested in accordance with section 5 of BS 5852:1990;
- curtains, hangings and temporary decorations are arranged so as not to obstruct exits, fire safety signs or fire-fighting equipment; and
- temporary decorations are not used without prior notification to the licensing authority/fire authority.

Accommodation limits

In certain premises where existing legislation does not provide adequately for the safety of the public or club members and guests, consideration might also be given to conditions that ensure that:

- arrangements are made to ensure that any capacity limit imposed under the premises licence or club premises certificate are not exceeded; and
- the licence holder, a club official, manager or designated premises supervisor should be aware of the number of people on the premises and required to inform any authorised person on request.

Fire action notices

In certain premises where existing legislation does not provide adequately for the safety of the public or club members and guests, consideration might also be given to conditions that ensure that:

- notices detailing the actions to be taken in the event of fire or other emergencies, including how the fire brigade should be summoned, are prominently displayed and protected from damage and deterioration.

Outbreaks of fire

In certain premises where existing legislation does not provide adequately for the safety of the public or club members and guests, consideration might also be given to conditions that ensure that:

- the fire brigade must be called at once to any outbreak of fire, however slight, and the details recorded in a Fire Log-book.

Loss of water

In certain premises where existing legislation does not provide adequately for the safety of the public or club members and guests, consideration might also be given to conditions that ensure that:

- the local Fire Control Centre are notified as soon as possible if the water supply to any hydrant, hose reel, sprinkler, drencher or other fire extinguishing installation is cut off or restricted.

Access for emergency vehicles

In certain premises where existing legislation does not provide adequately for the safety of the public or club members and guests, consideration might also be given to conditions that ensure that:

- access for emergency vehicles is kept clear and free from obstruction.

First aid

In certain premises where existing legislation does not provide adequately for the safety of the public or club members and guests, consideration might also be given to conditions that ensure that:

- adequate and appropriate supply of first aid equipment and materials is available on the premises;
- if necessary, at least one suitably trained first-aider shall be on duty when the public are present; and if more than one suitably trained first-aider that their respective duties are clearly defined.

Lighting

In certain premises where existing legislation does not provide adequately for the safety of the public or club members and guests, consideration might also be given to conditions that ensure that:

- in the absence of adequate daylight, the lighting in any area accessible to the public, members or guests shall be fully in operation when they are present;
- fire safety signs are adequately illuminated;
- emergency lighting is not altered;
- emergency lighting batteries are fully charged before the admission of the public, members or guests; and

- in the event of the failure of normal lighting, where the emergency lighting battery has a capacity of one hour, arrangements are in place to ensure that the public, members or guests leave the premises within 20 minutes unless within that time normal lighting has been restored and the battery is being re-charged; and, if the emergency lighting battery has a capacity of three hours, the appropriate period by the end of which the public should have left the premises is one hour.

Temporary electrical installations

In certain premises where existing legislation does not provide adequately for the safety of the public or club members and guests, consideration might also be given to conditions that ensure that:

- temporary electrical wiring and distribution systems are not provided without [notification to the licensing authority at least ten days before commencement of the work] [prior inspection by a suitable qualified electrician];
- temporary electrical wiring and distribution systems shall comply with the recommendations of BS 7671 or where applicable BS 7909; and
- where they have not been installed by a competent person, temporary electrical wiring and distribution systems are inspected and certified by a competent person before they are put to use.

With regard to the first bullet above, it should be recognised that ten days notice may not be possible where performances are supported by outside technical teams. For example, where temporary electrical installations are made in theatres for television show performances. In such circumstances, the key requirement is that conditions where necessary should ensure that temporary electrical installations are only undertaken by competent qualified persons, for example, employed by the television company.

Indoor sports entertainments

In certain premises where existing legislation does not provide adequately for the safety of the public or club members and guests, consideration might also be given to conditions that ensure that:

- if necessary, an appropriately qualified medical practitioner is present throughout a sports entertainment involving boxing, wrestling, judo, karate or other sports entertainment of a similar nature;
- where a ring is involved, it is constructed and supported by a competent person and inspected by a competent authority and any material used to form the skirt around the ring is flame-retardant;
- at any wrestling or other entertainments of a similar nature members of the public do not occupy any seat within 2.5 metres of the ring; and
- at water sports entertainments, staff adequately trained in rescue and life safety procedures are stationed and remain within the vicinity of the water at all material times (see also Managing Health and Safety in Swimming Pools issued jointly by the Health and Safety Commission and Sport England).

Alterations to the premises

Premises should not be altered in such a way as to make it impossible to comply with an existing licence condition without first seeking a variation of the premises licence proposing the deletion of the condition relating to public safety in question. The applicant will need to propose in a new operating schedule reflecting the proposed alteration to the premises how he or she intends to take alternative steps to promote the public safety objective. The application for variation will enable the responsible authorities with expertise in safety matters to consider whether the proposal is acceptable.

Special effects

The use of special effects in venues of all kinds being used for regulated entertainment is increasingly common and can present significant risks. Any special effects or mechanical installation should be arranged and stored so as to minimise any risk to the safety of the audience, the performers and staff.

Specials effects which should be considered include:

- dry ice machines and cryogenic fog;
- smoke machines and fog generators;
- pyrotechnics, including fireworks;
- real flame;
- firearms;
- motor vehicles;
- strobe lighting;
- lasers (see HSE Guide The Radiation Safety of lasers used for display purposes [HS(G)95] and BS EN 60825: Safety of laser products);
- explosives and highly flammable substances.

In certain circumstances, it may be necessary to require that certain special effects are only used with the prior notification of the licensing authority or [inspection by] the fire authority.

Annex G

Conditions relating to the prevention of public nuisance

It should be noted that provisions of the Environmental Protection Act 1990 and the Noise Act 1996 provide some protection to the general public from the effects of noise nuisance. In addition, the provisions in Part 8 of the Licensing Act 2003 enable a senior police officer to close down instantly for up to 24 hours licensed premises and premises carrying on temporary permitted activities that are causing nuisance resulting from noise emanating from the premises. These matters should be considered before deciding whether or not conditions are necessary for the prevention of public nuisance.

General

When applicants for premises licences or club premises certificates are preparing their operating schedules or club operating schedules, responsible authorities are considering such applications and licensing authorities are considering applications following the receipt of relevant representations from a responsible authority or interested party, the following options should be considered as measures that, if necessary, would promote the prevention of public nuisance.

Whether or not any risk assessment shows them to be necessary in the individual circumstances of any premises will depend on a range of factors including the nature and style of the venue, the activities being conducted there, the location of the premises and the anticipated clientele of the business involved.

Necessary conditions for licences and certificates will also depend on local knowledge of the premises.

Hours

The hours during which the premises are permitted to be open to the public or to members and their

114

guests can be restricted (other than where they are protected by the transitional provisions of the Licensing Act 2003) by the conditions of a premises licence or a club premises certificate for the prevention of public nuisance. But this must be balanced by the potential impact on disorder which results from artificially early fixed closing times.

Restrictions could be necessary on the times when certain licensable activities take place even though the premises may be open to the public at such times. For example, the playing of recorded music after a certain time might be prohibited, even though other licensable activities are permitted to continue.

Restrictions might be necessary on the parts of premises that might be used for certain licensable activities at certain times. For example, while the provision of regulated entertainment might be permitted while the premises is open to the public or members and their guests, regulated entertainment might not be permitted in garden areas of the premises after a certain time.

Noise and vibration

In certain premises where existing legislation does not provide adequately for the prevention of public nuisance, consideration might be given to conditions that ensure that:

- noise or vibration does not emanate from the premises so as to cause a nuisance to nearby properties. This might be achieved by a simple requirement to keep doors and windows at the premises closed, or to use noise limiters on amplification equipment used at the premises;
- prominent, clear and legible notices are displayed at all exits requesting the public to respect the needs of local residents and to leave the premises and the area quietly;
- the use of explosives, pyrotechnics and fireworks of a similar nature which could cause disturbance in surrounding areas are restricted; and
- the placing of refuse – such as bottles – into receptacles outside the premises takes place at times that will minimise the disturbance to nearby properties.

Noxious smells

In certain premises where existing legislation does not provide adequately for the prevention of public nuisance, consideration might be given to conditions that ensure that:

- noxious smells from licensed premises are not permitted so as to cause a nuisance to nearby properties and the premises are properly vented.

Light pollution

In certain premises where existing legislation does not provide adequately for the prevention of public nuisance, consideration might be given to conditions that ensure that:

- flashing or particularly bright lights on or outside licensed premises do not cause a nuisance to nearby properties. Any such condition needs to be balanced against the benefits to the prevention of crime and disorder of bright lighting in certain places.

Annex H

Conditions relating to the protection of children from harm

It should be noted that it is unlawful under the 2003 Act to permit unaccompanied children under the age of 16 to be present on premises exclusively or primarily used for supply of alcohol for consumption on those premises under the authorisation of a premises licence, club premises certificate or a temporary event notice when open for the purposes of being used for the supply of alcohol for consumption there. In addition, it is an offence to permit the presence of children under 16 who are not accompanied by an adult between midnight and 5am at all premises supplying alcohol for consumption on those premises under the authorisation of any premises licence, club premises certificate or temporary event notice. Conditions duplicating these provisions are, therefore, unnecessary.

Access for children to licensed premises – in general

Restrictions on the access of children under 18 to premises where licensable activities are being carried on should be made where it is necessary to protect children from harm. Precise policy and details will be a matter for individual licensing authorities. Conditions attached to premises licences and club premises certificates may reflect the concerns of responsible authorities and interested parties who have made representations but only where the licensing authority considers it necessary to protect children from harm. Whilst applications in relation to premises licences and club premises certificates must be judged by licensing authorities on their individual merits and characteristics, the Secretary of State recommends (unless there are circumstances justifying the contrary) that:

- for any premises with known associations (having been presented with evidence) with or likely to give rise to heavy or binge or underage drinking, drugs, significant gambling, or any activity or entertainment (whether regulated entertainment or not) of a clearly adult or sexual nature, there should be a strong presumption against permitting any access at all for children under 18 years. Applicants wishing to allow access for children to premises where these associations may be relevant, when preparing operating schedules or club operating schedules or variations of those schedules for the purposes of obtaining or varying a premises licence or club premises certificate should:
  - explain their reasons; and
  - outline in detail the steps that they intend to take to protect children from harm on such premises.

- for any premises, not serving alcohol for consumption on the premises, but where the public are allowed on the premises after 11.00pm in the evening, there should be a presumption against the presence of children under the age of 12 unaccompanied by adults after that time. Applicants wishing to allow access when preparing operating schedules or variations of those schedules or club operating schedules for the purposes of obtaining or varying a premises licence or club premises certificate should:
  - explain their reasons; and
  - outline in detail the steps that they intend to take to protect children from harm on such premises.

- in any other case, subject to the premises licence holder's or club's discretion, the expectation would be for unrestricted access for children subject to the terms of the 2003 Act. An operating schedule or club operating schedule should indicate any decision for the premises to exclude children completely, which would mean there would be no need to detail in the operating schedule steps that the applicant proposes to take to promote the protection of children from harm. Otherwise, where entry is to be permitted, the operating schedule should outline the steps to be taken to promote the protection of children from harm while on the premises.

Age Restrictions – specific

Under the 2003 Act a wide variety of licensable activities could take place at various types of premises and at different times of the day and night. Whilst it may be appropriate to allow children unrestricted access at particular times and when certain activities are not taking place, licensing authorities following relevant representations made by responsible authorities and interested parties will need to consider a range of conditions that are to be tailored to the particular premises and their activities where these are necessary. Licensing authorities are expected to consider:

- the hours of day during which age restrictions should and should not apply. For example, the fact that adult entertainment may be presented at premises after 8.00pm does not mean that it would be necessary to impose age restrictions for earlier parts of the day;

- types of event or activity in respect of which no age restrictions may be needed, for example;
  - family entertainment; or
  - non-alcohol events for young age groups, such as under 18s dances,

- Similarly, types of event or activity which give rise to a more acute need for age restrictions than normal, for example;
  - during "Happy Hours" or on drinks promotion nights;
  - during activities outlined in the first bullet point in the first paragraph above.

Age restrictions – cinemas

The Secretary of State considers that, in addition to the mandatory condition imposed by virtue of section 20, requiring the admission of children to films to be restricted in accordance with recommendations given either by a body designated under section 4 of the Video Recordings Act 1984 or by the licensing authority itself, conditions restricting the admission of children to film exhibitions should include:

- a condition that where the licensing authority itself is to make recommendations on the admission of children to films, the cinema or venue operator must submit any film to the authority that it intends to exhibit 28 days before it is proposed to show it. This is to allow the authority time to classify it so that the premises licence holder is able to adhere to any age restrictions then imposed;

- a condition that when films are classified, by either the film classification body as specified in the licence or the licensing authority, they should be classified in the following way:
  - U – Universal. Suitable for audiences aged four years and over.
  - PG – Parental Guidance. Some scenes may be unsuitable for young children.
  - 12A – Passed only for viewing by persons aged 12 years or older or persons younger than 12 when accompanied by an adult.
  - 15 – Passed only for viewing by persons aged 15 years and over.
  - 18 – Passed only for viewing by persons aged 18 years and over.

- that conditions specify that immediately before each exhibition at the premises of a film passed by the British Board of Film Classification there shall be exhibited on screen for at least five seconds in such a manner as to be easily read by all persons in the auditorium a reproduction of the certificate of the Board or, as regards a trailer advertising a film, of the statement approved by the Board indicating the classification of the film;

- a condition that when a licensing authority has made a recommendation on the restriction of admission of children to a film, notices are required to be displayed both inside and outside the premises so that persons entering can readily be made aware of the classification attached to any film or trailer. Such a condition might be expressed in the following terms:

"Where a programme includes a film recommended by the licensing authority as falling into the 12A, 15 or 18 category no person appearing to be under the age of 12 and unaccompanied, or under 15 or 18 as appropriate, shall be admitted to any part of the programme; and the licence holder shall display in a conspicuous position a notice in the following terms –

PERSONS UNDER THE AGE OF [INSERT APPROPRIATE AGE] CANNOT BE ADMITTED TO ANY PART OF THE PROGRAMME

Where films of different categories form part of the same programme, the notice shall refer to the oldest age restriction.

This condition does not apply to members of staff under the relevant age while on-duty provided that the prior written consent of the person's parent or legal guardian has first been obtained."

Theatres

The admission of children to theatres, as with other licensed premises, is not expected to normally be restricted unless it is necessary to promote the licensing objective of the protection of children from harm. However, theatres may be the venue for a wide range of activities. The admission of children to the performance of a play is expected to normally be left to the discretion of the licence holder and no condition restricting the access of children to plays should be attached. However, theatres may also present entertainment including, for example, variety shows, incorporating adult entertainment. A condition restricting the admission of children in such circumstances may be necessary. Entertainment may also be presented at theatres specifically for children (see below).

Licensing authorities are also expected to consider whether a condition should be attached to a premises licence which requires the presence of a sufficient number of adult staff on the premises to ensure the well being of children present on the premises during any emergency (See Annex F).

Performances especially for children

Where performances are presented especially for unaccompanied children in theatres and cinemas conditions are anticipated to be needed which require:

Children in performances

There are many productions each year that are one-off shows where the cast is made up almost entirely of children. They may be taking part as individuals or as part of a drama club, stage school or school group. The age of those involved may range from 5 to 18. The Children (Performances) Regulations 1968 as amended set out requirements for children performing in a show. Licensing authorities should familiarise themselves with the requirements of these Regulations and not duplicate any of these requirements. However, if it is necessary to consider imposing conditions, in addition to these requirements, for the promotion of the protection of children from harm then the licensing authority should consider the matters outlined below.

- **Venue** – the backstage facilities should be large enough to accommodate safely the number of children taking part in any performance.
- **Fire safety** – all chaperones and production crew on the show should receive instruction on the fire procedures applicable to the venue prior to the arrival of the children.

- **Special effects** – it may be inappropriate to use certain special effects, including smoke, dry ice, rapid pulsating or flashing lights, which may trigger adverse reactions especially with regard to children.
- **Care of children** – theatres, concert halls and similar places are places of work and may contain a lot of potentially dangerous equipment. It is therefore important that children performing at such premises are kept under adult supervision at all times including transfer from stage to dressing room and anywhere else on the premises. It is also important that the children can be accounted for at all times in case of an evacuation or emergency.

The Portman Group Code of Practice on the Naming, Packaging and Promotion of Alcoholic Drinks

The Portman Group operates, on behalf of the alcohol industry, a Code of Practice on the Naming, Packaging and Promotion of Alcoholic Drinks. The Code seeks to ensure that drinks are packaged and promoted in a socially responsible manner and only to those who are 18 years old or older. Complaints about products under the Code are considered by an Independent Complaints Panel and the Panel's decisions are published on the Portman Group's website, in the trade press and in an annual report. If a product's packaging or point-of-sale advertising is found to be in breach of the Code, the Portman Group may issue a Retailer Alert Bulletin to notify retailers of the decision and ask them not to replenish stocks of any such product or to display such point-of-sale material, until the decision has been complied with. The Code is an important mechanism in protecting children from harm because it addresses the naming, marketing and promotion of alcohol products sold in licensed premises in a manner which may appeal to or attract minors.

Where appropriate and necessary, consideration can be given to attaching conditions to premises licences and club premises certificates that require compliance with the Portman Group's Retailer Alert Bulletins.

Proof of Age cards

Proof of age cards are discussed under Annex D in connection with the prevention of crime and disorder. However, where necessary and appropriate, a requirement for the production of proof of age cards before any sale of alcohol is made could be attached to any premises licence or club premises certificate for the protection of children from harm. Any such requirement should not be limited to recognised "proof of age" cards, but allow for the production of other proof, such as photo-driving licences and passports. The Secretary of State strongly supports the PASS accreditation system (see paragraph 12.8 of the Guidance) which aims to approve and accredit various proof of age schemes that are in existence. This ensures that such schemes maintain high standards, particularly in the area of integrity and security, and where appropriate and necessary, conditions may refer directly to PASS accredited proof of age cards, photo-driving licences, student cards and passports. As for conditions relating to crime and disorder, it should be noted that many adults in England and Wales do not currently carry any proof of age. This means that the wording of any condition will require careful thought. For example, the requirement might be to ensure sight of evidence of age from any person appearing to those engaged in selling or supplying alcohol to be under the age of 18 and who is attempting to buy alcohol. This would ensure that most minors – even those looking older – would need to produce proof of age appropriately before making such a purchase. Under such an arrangement only a minority of adults might be affected, but for the majority there would be no disruption to their normal activity, for example, when shopping in a supermarket.

Proof of age cards can also ensure that appropriate checks are made where the presence of children is restricted by age at certain times, such as 16.

119

USEFUL WEBSITES

Association of Licensed Multiple Retailers: trade body dedicated to representing interest of pub and bar operators and other licensed retailers. www.almr.org.uk

Bar Entertainment and Dance Association: representing late night venues throughout the UK. www.beda.org.uk

British Beer and Pub Association: leading organisation representing the brewing and pub sector. www.beerandpub.com

British Hospitality and Restaurant Association: national trade association for hotel, foodservice, catering and leisure sectors. www.bha-online.org.uk

British Institute of Innkeeping: professional body for the licensed trade. www.bii.org.uk

City and Guilds: www.city-guilds.co.uk

Committee of Registered Clubs Association: leading forum for non-profit making private members' clubs. www.wmciu.org.uk

Department for Culture, Media and Sport: government department website where the Guidance plus various application forms and notices may be downloaded. www.culture.gov.uk.
For enquiries regarding alcohol & entertainment licensing email: alcohol.entertainment@culture.gov.uk

Disclosure Scotland: www.disclosurescotland.co.uk

Federation of Licensed Victuallers Associations: members' organisation which looks after the interests of self-employed licensees. www.flva.co.uk

Guild of Master Victuallers: body representing self-employed licensees who are generally single operators. Enquiries to sharp-bill @hotmail.com

Licensed Victuallers of Wales: non-profit making organisation promoting interests of its self-employed, on-licence members. Enquiries to gjohnlvwales@hotmail.com

Local Government Association: national voice for local communities speaking for nearly 500 local authorities. www.lga.gov.uk

Security Industry Authority: www.the-sia.org.uk